Python Artificial Intelligence Projects for Beginners

Get up and running with Artificial Intelligence using 8 smart and exciting AI applications

Joshua Eckroth

BIRMINGHAM - MUMBAI

Python Artificial Intelligence Projects for Beginners

Commissioning Editor: Pravin Dhandre
Acquisition Editor: Joshua Nadar
Content Development Editors: Prasad Ramesh, Karan Thakkar
Technical Editor: Sagar Sawant
Copy Editor: Safis Editing
Project Coordinator: Nidhi Joshi
Proofreader: Safis Editing
Indexer: Pratik Shirodkar
Graphics: Jisha Chirayil
Production Coordinator: Arvindkumar Gupta

First published: July 2018

Production reference: 1300718

Published by Packt Publishing Ltd.
Livery Place
35 Livery Street
Birmingham
B3 2PB, UK.

ISBN 978-1-78953-946-2

www.packtpub.com

`mapt.io`

Mapt is an online digital library that gives you full access to over 5,000 books and videos, as well as industry leading tools to help you plan your personal development and advance your career. For more information, please visit our website.

Why subscribe?

- Spend less time learning and more time coding with practical eBooks and Videos from over 4,000 industry professionals

- Improve your learning with Skill Plans built especially for you

- Get a free eBook or video every month

- Mapt is fully searchable

- Copy and paste, print, and bookmark content

PacktPub.com

Did you know that Packt offers eBook versions of every book published, with PDF and ePub files available? You can upgrade to the eBook version at `www.PacktPub.com` and as a print book customer, you are entitled to a discount on the eBook copy. Get in touch with us at `service@packtpub.com` for more details.

At `www.PacktPub.com`, you can also read a collection of free technical articles, sign up for a range of free newsletters, and receive exclusive discounts and offers on Packt books and eBooks.

Contributors

About the author

Joshua Eckroth is assistant professor of computer science at Stetson University, where he teaches big data mining and analytics, artificial intelligence (AI), and software engineering. Dr. Eckroth joined the math and computer science department at Stetson University in fall 2014. He earned his PhD from Ohio State University in AI and cognitive science, focusing on abductive reasoning and meta-reasoning.

Packt is searching for authors like you

If you're interested in becoming an author for Packt, please visit authors.packtpub.com and apply today. We have worked with thousands of developers and tech professionals, just like you, to help them share their insight with the global tech community. You can make a general application, apply for a specific hot topic that we are recruiting an author for, or submit your own idea.

Table of Contents

Preface

Artificial Intelligence (AI) is the newest emerging and disruptive technology among varied businesses, industries, and sectors. This book demonstrates AI projects in Python, covering modern techniques that make up the world of AI.

This book begins with building your first prediction model using the popular Python library, scikit-learn. You will understand how to build a classifier using effective machine learning techniques: random forest and decision trees. With exciting projects on predicting bird species, analyzing student performance data, song genre identification, and spam detection, you will learn the fundamentals and various algorithms and techniques that foster the development of such smart applications. You will also understand deep learning and the neural network mechanism through these projects with the use of the Keras library.

By the end of this book, you will be confident to build your own AI projects with Python and be ready to take on more advanced content as you go ahead.

Who this book is for

This book is for Python developers who want to take their first step in the world of artificial intelligence using easy-to-follow projects. Basic working knowledge of Python programming is expected so that you can play around with the code.

What this book covers

Chapter 1, *Building Your Own Prediction Models*, introduces classification and techniques for evaluation, and then explains decision trees, followed by a coding project in which a predictor for student performance is built.

Chapter 2, *Prediction with Random Forests*, looks at random forests and uses them in a coding project for classifying bird species.

Chapter 3, *Applications for Comment Classification*, introduces text processing and the bag-of-words technique. Then shows how this technique can be used to build a spam detector for YouTube comments. Next, you will learn about the sophisticated Word2Vec model and practice it with a coding project that detects positive and negative product, restaurant, and movie reviews.

Chapter 4, *Neural Networks*, covers a brief introduction to neural networks, proceeds with feedforward neural networks, and looks at a program to identify the genre of a song with neural networks. Finally, you will revise the spam detector from earlier to make it work with neural networks.

Chapter 5, *Deep Learning*, discusses deep learning and CNNs. You will practice convolutional neural networks and deep learning with two projects. First, you will build a system that can read handwritten mathematical symbols and then revisit the bird species identifier and change the implementation to use a deep convolutional neural network that is significantly more accurate.

To get the most out of this book

1. You need to have a basic understanding of Python and its scientific computing libraries
2. Get Jupyter Notebook installed, preferably via Anaconda

Download the example code files

You can download the example code files for this book from your account at www.packtpub.com. If you purchased this book elsewhere, you can visit www.packtpub.com/support and register to have the files emailed directly to you.

You can download the code files by following these steps:

1. Log in or register at www.packtpub.com.
2. Select the **SUPPORT** tab.
3. Click on **Code Downloads & Errata**.
4. Enter the name of the book in the **Search** box and follow the onscreen instructions.

Once the file is downloaded, please make sure that you unzip or extract the folder using the latest version of:

*   WinRAR/7-Zip for Windows
*   Zipeg/iZip/UnRarX for Mac
*   7-Zip/PeaZip for Linux

The code bundle for the book is also hosted on GitHub
at https://github.com/PacktPublishing/Python-Artificial-Intelligence-Projects-for-Beginners. In case there's an update to the code, it will be updated on the existing
GitHub repository.

We also have other code bundles from our rich catalog of books and videos available
at https://github.com/PacktPublishing/. Check them out!

Download the color images

We also provide a PDF file that has color images of the screenshots/diagrams used in this
book. You can download it here: http://www.packtpub.com/sites/default/files/
downloads/PythonArtificialIntelligenceProjectsforBeginners_ColorImages.pdf.

Conventions used

There are a number of text conventions used throughout this book.

CodeInText: Indicates code words in text, database table names, folder names, filenames,
file extensions, pathnames, dummy URLs, user input, and Twitter handles. Here is an
example: "The classes.txt file shows class IDs with the bird species names."

Bold: Indicates a new term, an important word, or words that you see onscreen. For
example, words in menus or dialog boxes appear in the text like this.

Warnings or important notes appear like this.

Tips and tricks appear like this.

Get in touch

Feedback from our readers is always welcome.

General feedback: Email `feedback@packtpub.com` and mention the book title in the subject of your message. If you have questions about any aspect of this book, please email us at `questions@packtpub.com`.

Errata: Although we have taken every care to ensure the accuracy of our content, mistakes do happen. If you have found a mistake in this book, we would be grateful if you would report this to us. Please visit `www.packtpub.com/submit-errata`, selecting your book, clicking on the Errata Submission Form link, and entering the details.

Piracy: If you come across any illegal copies of our works in any form on the Internet, we would be grateful if you would provide us with the location address or website name. Please contact us at `copyright@packtpub.com` with a link to the material.

If you are interested in becoming an author: If there is a topic that you have expertise in and you are interested in either writing or contributing to a book, please visit `authors.packtpub.com`.

Reviews

Please leave a review. Once you have read and used this book, why not leave a review on the site that you purchased it from? Potential readers can then see and use your unbiased opinion to make purchase decisions, we at Packt can understand what you think about our products, and our authors can see your feedback on their book. Thank you!

For more information about Packt, please visit `packtpub.com`.

Building Your Own Prediction Models

1

Our society is more technologically advanced than ever. **Artificial Intelligence (AI)** technology is already spreading throughout the world, replicating humankind. The intention of creating machines that could emulate aspects of human intelligence such as reasoning, learning, and problem solving gave birth to the development of AI technology. AI truly rivals human nature. In other words, AI makes a machine think and behave like a human. An example that can best demonstrate the power of this technology would be the tag suggestions or face-recognition feature of Facebook. Looking at the tremendous impact of this technology on today's world, AI will definitely become one of the greatest technologies out there in the coming years.

We are going to be experimenting with a project based on AI technology, exploring classification using machine learning algorithms along with the Python programming language. We will also explore a few examples for a better understanding.

In this chapter, we are going to explore the following interesting topics:

- An overview of the classification technique
- The Python scikit library

Classification overview and evaluation techniques

AI provides us with various amazing classification techniques, but machine learning classification would be the best to start with as it is the most common and easiest classification to understand for the beginner. In our daily life, our eyes captures millions of pictures: be they in a book, on a particular screen, or maybe something that you caught in your surroundings. These images captured by our eyes help us to recognize and classify objects. Our application is based on the same logic.

Here, we are creating an application that will identify images using machine learning algorithms. Imagine that we have images of both apples and oranges, looking at which our application would help identify whether the image is of an apple or an orange. This type of classification can be termed as **binary classification**, which means classifying the objects of a given set into two groups, but techniques do exist for multiclass classification as well. We would require a large number of images of apples and oranges, and a machine learning algorithm that would be set in such a way that the application would be able to classify both image types. In other words, we make these algorithms learn the difference between the two objects to help classify all the examples correctly. This is known as **supervised learning**.

Now let's compare supervised learning with unsupervised learning. Let's assume that we are not aware of the actual data labels (which means we do not know whether the images are examples of apples or oranges). In such cases, classification won't be of much help. The **clustering** method can always ease such scenarios. The result would be a model that can be deployed in an application, and it would function as seen in the following diagram. The application would memorize facts about the distinction between apples and oranges and recognize actual images using a machine learning algorithm. If we took a new input, the model would tell us about its decision as to whether the input is an apple or orange. In this example, the application that we created is able to identify an image of an apple with a 75% degree of confidence:

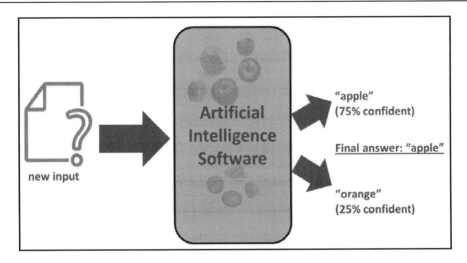

Sometimes, we want to know the level of confidence, and other times we just want the final answer, that is, the choice in which the model has the most confidence.

Evaluation

We can evaluate how well the model is working by measuring its accuracy. Accuracy would be defined as the percentage of cases that are classified correctly. We can analyze the mistakes made by the model, or its level of confusion, using a confusion matrix. The confusion matrix refers to the confusion in the model, but these confusion matrices can become a little difficult to understand when they become very large. Let's take a look at the following binary classification example, which shows the number of times that the model has made the correct predictions of the object:

	Predicted "apple"	Predicted "orange"
True "apple"	20	5
True "orange"	3	22

In the preceding table, the rows of **True apple** and **True orange** refers to cases where the object was actually an apple or actually an orange. The columns refer to the prediction made by the model. We see that in our example, there are 20 apples that were predicted correctly, while there were 5 apples that were wrongly identified as oranges.

Ideally, a confusion matrix should have all zeros, except for the diagonal. Here we can calculate the accuracy by adding the figures diagonally, so that these are all the correctly classified examples, and dividing that sum by the sum of all the numbers in the matrix:

$$Accuracy = (20 + 22)/20 + 5 + 3 + 22) = 84$$

Here we got the accuracy as 84%. To know more about confusion matrices, let's go through another example, which involves three classes, as seen in the following diagram:

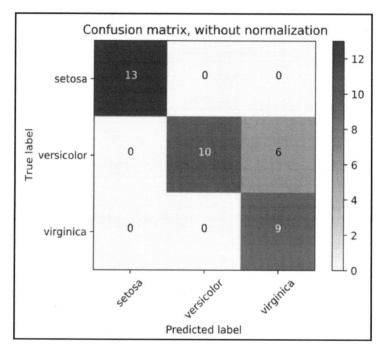

Source: scikit-learn docs

There are three different species of iris flowers. The matrix gives raw accounts of correct and incorrect predictions. So, **setosa** was correctly predicted 13 times out of all the examples of setosa images from the dataset. On the other hand, **versicolor** was predicted correctly on 10 occasions, and there were 6 occasions where versicolor was predicted as **virginica.** Now let's normalize our confusion matrix and show the percentage of the cases that predicted image corrected or incorrectly. In our example we saw that the setosa species was predicted correctly throughout:

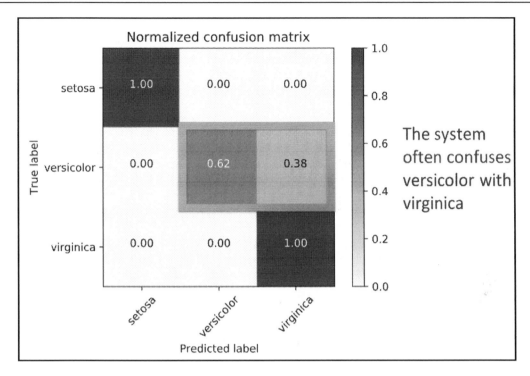

The system often confuses versicolor with virginica

Source: scikit-learn docs

During evaluation of the confusion matrix, we also saw that the system got confused between two species: versicolor and virginica. This also gives us the conclusion that the system is not able to identify species of virginica all the time.

For further instances, we need to be more aware that we cannot have really high accuracy since the system will be trained and tested on the same data. This will lead to memorizing the training set and overfitting of the model. Therefore, we should try to split the data into training and testing sets, first in either 90/10% or 80/20%. Then we should use the training set for developing the model and the test set for performing and calculating the accuracy of the confusion matrix.

We need to be careful not to choose a really good testing set or a really bad testing set to get the accuracy. Hence to be sure we use a validation known as **K-fold cross validation**. To understand it a bit better, imagine 5-fold cross validation, where we move the testing set by 20 since there are 5 rows. Then we move the remaining set with the dataset and find the average of all the folds:

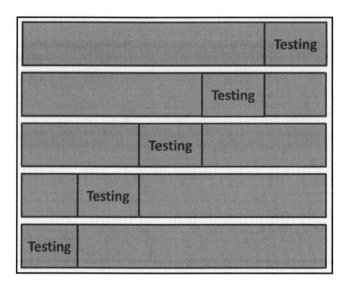

Quite confusing, right? But scikit-learn has built-in support for cross validation. This feature will be a good way to make sure that we are not overfitting our model and we are not running our model on a bad testing set.

Decision trees

In this section, we will be using decision trees and student performance data to predict whether a child will do well in school. We will use the previous techniques with some scikit-learn code. Before starting with the prediction, let's just learn a bit about what decision trees are.

Decision trees are one of the simplest techniques for classification. They can be compared with a game of **20 questions**, where each node in the tree is either a leaf node or a question node. Consider the case of Titanic survivability, which was built from a dataset that includes data on the survival outcome of each passenger of the Titanic.

Consider our first node as a question: *Is the passenger a male?* If not, then the passenger most likely survived. Otherwise, we would have another question to ask about the male passengers: *Was the male over the age of 9.5?* (where 9.5 was chosen by the decision tree learning procedure as an ideal split of the data). If the answer is **Yes**, then the passenger most likely did not survive. If the answer is **No**, then it will raise another question: *Is the passenger a sibling?* The following diagram will give you a brief explanation:

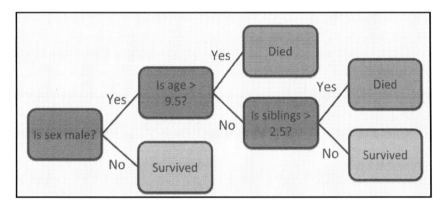

Understanding the decision trees does not require you to be an expert in the decision tree learning process. As seen in the previous diagram, the process makes understanding data very simple. Not all machine learning models are as easy to understand as decision trees.

Let us now dive deep into decision tree by knowing more about decision tree learning process. Considering the same titanic dataset we used earlier, we will find the best attribute to split on according to information gain, which is also known as **entropy**:

survived	class	sex	age	spouse/siblings	parents/children
1	1	female	29	0	0
1	1	male	0.9	1	2
0	1	female	2	1	2
0	1	male	30	1	2
0	1	female	25	1	2
1	1	male	48	0	0
1	1	female	63	1	0
0	1	male	39	0	0
1	1	female	53	2	0
0	1	male	71	0	0
0	1	male	47	1	0
1	1	female	18	1	0
1	1	female	24	0	0
1	1	female	26	0	0
1	1	male	80	0	0

Information gain is highest only when the outcome is more predictable after knowing the value in a certain column. In other words, if we know whether the passenger is **male** or **female**, we will know whether he or she survived, hence the information gain is highest for the sex column. We do not consider age column best for our first split since we do not know much about the passengers ages, and is not the best first split because we will know less about the outcome if all we know is a passenger's age.

After splitting on the **sex** column according to the information gain, what we have now is **female** and **male** subsets, as seen in the following screenshot:

		Find next best attribute on subset						Find next best attribute on subset			
survived	class	sex	age	spouse/siblings	parents/children	survived	class	sex	age	spouse/siblings	parents/children
1	1	female	29	0	0	1	1	male	0.9	1	2
0	1	female	2	1	2	0	1	male	30	1	2
0	1	female	25	1	2	1	1	male	48	0	0
1	1	female	63	1	0	0	1	male	39	0	0
1	1	female	53	2	0	0	1	male	71	0	0
1	1	female	18	1	0	0	1	male	47	1	0
1	1	female	24	0	0	1	1	male	80	0	0
1	1	female	26	0	0	0	1	male		0	0
1	1	female	50	0	1	0	1	male	24	0	1
1	1	female	32	0	0	0	1	male	36	0	0
1	1	female	47	1	1	1	1	male	37	1	1

After the split, we have one internode and one question node, as seen in the previous screenshot, and two paths that can be taken depending on the answer to the question. Now we need to find the best attribute again in both of the subsets. The left subset, in which all passengers are female, does not have a good attribute to split on because many passengers survived. Hence, the left subset just turns into a leaf node that predicts survival. On the right-hand side, the `age` attribute is chosen as the best split, considering the value **9.5** years of age as the split. We gain two more subsets: age greater than **9.5** and age lower than **9.5**:

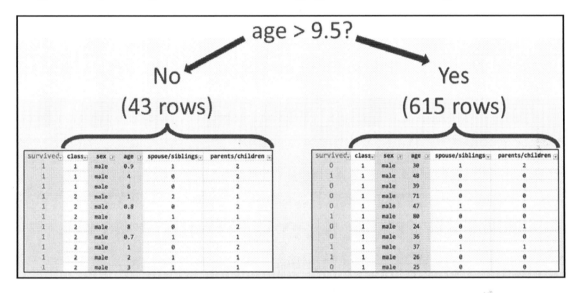

Repeat the process of splitting the data into two new subsets until there are no good splits, or no remaining attributes, and leaf nodes are formed instead of question nodes. Before we start with our prediction model, let us know a little more about the scikit-learn package.

Common APIs for scikit-learn classifiers

In this section, we will be learn how to create code using the scikit-learn package to build and test decision trees. Scikit-learn contains many simple sets of functions. In fact, except for the second line of code that you can see in the following screenshot, which is specifically about decision trees, we will use the same functions for other classifiers as well, such as random forests:

```
from sklearn import tree
t = tree.DecisionTreeClassifier(criterion="entropy")

t = t.fit(train_attributes, train_labels)        Build the decision tree

t.score(test_attributes, test_labels)            Build the decision tree

t.predict(example_attributes)                    Predict a new example

cross_val_score(t, all_attributes, all_labels)   Average scores with
                                                 cross-validation
```

Before we jump further into technical part, let's try to understand what the lines of code mean. The first two lines of code are used to set a decision tree, but we can consider this as not yet built as we have not pointed the tree to any trained set. The third line builds the tree using the `fit` function. Next, we score a list of examples and obtain an accuracy number. These two lines of code will be used to build the decision tree. After which, we predict function with a single example, which means we will take a row of data to train the model and predict the output with the survived column. Finally, we runs cross-validation, splitting the data and building an entry for each training split and evaluating the tree for each testing split. On running these code the result we have are the scores and the we average the scores.

Here you will have a question: *When should we use decision trees?* The answer to this can be quite simple as decision trees are simple and easy to interpret and require little data preparation, though you cannot consider them as the most accurate techniques. You can show the result of a decision tree to any subject matter expert, such as a Titanic historian (for our example). Even experts who know very little about machine learning would presumably be able to follow the tree's questions and gauge whether the tree is accurate.

Decision trees can perform better when the data has few attributes, but may perform poorly when the data has many attributes. This is because the tree may grow too large to be understandable and could easily overfit the training data by introducing branches that are too specific to the training data and don't really bear any relation to the test data created, this can reduce the chance of getting an accurate result. As, by now, you are aware of the basics of the decision tree, we are now ready to achieve our goal of creating a prediction model using student performance data.

Prediction involving decision trees and student performance data

In this section, we're going to use decision trees to predict student performance using the students, past performance data. We'll use the student performance dataset, which is available on the UC Irvine machine learning repository at `https://archive.ics.uci.edu/ml/datasets/student+performance`. Our final goal is to predict whether the student has passed or failed. The dataset contains the data of about 649 students, with and 30 attributes for each student. The attributes formed are mixed categorically – word and phrase, and numeric attributes. These mixed attributes cause a small problem that needs to be fixed. We will need to convert those word and phrase attributes into numbers.

The following screenshot shows the first half of the attributes from the data:

```
1 school - student's school (binary: 'GP' - Gabriel Pereira or 'MS' - Mousinho da Silveira)

2 sex - student's sex (binary: 'F' - female or 'M' - male)

3 age - student's age (numeric: from 15 to 22)

4 address - student's home address type (binary: 'U' - urban or 'R' - rural)

5 famsize - family size (binary: 'LE3' - less or equal to 3 or 'GT3' - greater than 3)

6 Pstatus - parent's cohabitation status (binary: 'T' - living together or 'A' - apart)

7 Medu - mother's education (numeric: 0 - none, 1 - primary education (4th grade), 2 - 5th to 9th grade, ...

8 Fedu - father's education (numeric: 0 - none, 1 - primary education (4th grade), 2 - 5th to 9th grade, ...

9 Mjob - mother's job (nominal: 'teacher', 'health' care related, civil 'services' (e.g. administrative or police), 'at_home' or 'other')

10 Fjob - father's job (nominal: 'teacher', 'health' care related, civil 'services' (e.g. administrative or police), 'at_home' or 'other')

11 reason - reason to choose this school (nominal: close to 'home', school 'reputation', 'course' preference or 'other')

12 guardian - student's guardian (nominal: 'mother', 'father' or 'other')

13 traveltime - home to school travel time (numeric: 1 - <15 min., 2 - 15 to 30 min., 3 - 30 min. to 1 hour, or 4 - >1 hour)

14 studytime - weekly study time (numeric: 1 - <2 hours, 2 - 2 to 5 hours, 3 - 5 to 10 hours, or 4 - >10 hours)

15 failures - number of past class failures (numeric: n if 1<=n<3, else 4)
```

You must have noticed how some of the attributes are categorical, such as the name of the school; **sex**; **Mjob**, which is the mother's occupation; **Fjob**, which is the father's occupation; reason; and guardian. Others, such as **age** and **traveltime**, are numeric. The following screenshot shows the second half of the attributes from the data:

```
16 schoolsup - extra educational support (binary: yes or no)

17 famsup - family educational support (binary: yes or no)

18 paid - extra paid classes within the course subject (Math or Portuguese) (binary: yes or no)

19 activities - extra-curricular activities (binary: yes or no)

20 nursery - attended nursery school (binary: yes or no)

21 higher - wants to take higher education (binary: yes or no)

22 internet - Internet access at home (binary: yes or no)

23 romantic - with a romantic relationship (binary: yes or no)

24 famrel - quality of family relationships (numeric: from 1 - very bad to 5 - excellent)

25 freetime - free time after school (numeric: from 1 - very low to 5 - very high)

26 goout - going out with friends (numeric: from 1 - very low to 5 - very high)

27 Dalc - workday alcohol consumption (numeric: from 1 - very low to 5 - very high)

28 Walc - weekend alcohol consumption (numeric: from 1 - very low to 5 - very high)

29 health - current health status (numeric: from 1 - very bad to 5 - very good)

30 absences - number of school absences (numeric: from 0 to 93)
```

It is clear that some of the attributes are better predictors, such as absences and the number of past failures, while others attributes are probably less predictive, such as whether or not the student is in a romantic relationship or whether the student's guardian is the mother, father, or someone else. The decision tree will attempt to identify the most important or predictive attributes using this information gain provided. We'll be able to look at the resulting tree and identify the most predictive attributes because the most predictive attributes will be the earliest questions.

The original dataset had three test scores: G1, G2, and G3. Where G1 would be first grade, G2 being the second grade, and G3 being the final grade. We will simplify the problem by just providing pass or fail. This can be done by adding these three scores and checking whether the sum is sufficiently large enough which is 35. That brings us to about a 50% split of students passing and failing, giving us a balanced dataset. Now let's look at the code:

```
In [1]:  # Load dataset (student Portuguese scores)
         import pandas as pd
         d = pd.read_csv('student-por.csv', sep=';')
         len(d)

Out[1]:  649
```

We import the dataset (`student-por.csv`), which comes with semicolons instead of commas; hence, we mention the separators as semicolons. To cross verify, we will find the number of rows in the dataset. Using the length variable, we can see that there are 649 rows.

Next we add columns for pass and fail. The data in these columns would contain 1 or 0, where 1 means pass and 0 means fail. We are going to do that by computing with every row what the sum of the test scores would be. This will be calculated as if the sum of three score is greater than or equal to 35, 1 is given to the student and failing to that rule 0 is given to the student.

We need to `apply` this rule on every row of the dataset, and this will be done using the `apply` function, which is a feature of Pandas. Here `axis=1` means use apply per row and `axis=0` would mean apply per column. The next line means that a variable needs to be dropped: either G1, G2, G3. The following screenshot of the code will provide you with an idea of what we just learned:

```
In [2]:  # generate binary label (pass/fail) based on G1+G2+G3 (test grades, each 0-20 pts); threshold for passing is sum>=30
         d['pass'] = d.apply(lambda row: 1 if (row['G1']+row['G2']+row['G3']) >= 35 else 0, axis=1)
         d = d.drop(['G1', 'G2', 'G3'], axis=1)
         d.head()
```

The following screenshot shows the first 5 rows of the dataset and 31 columns. There are 31 columns because we have all the attributes plus our pass and fail columns:

Out[2]:	school	sex	age	address	famsize	Pstatus	Medu	Fedu	Mjob	Fjob	...	internet	romantic	famrel	freetime	goout	Dalc	Walc	health	absences
0	GP	F	18	U	GT3	A	4	4	at_home	teacher	...	no	no	4	3	4	1	1	3	4
1	GP	F	17	U	GT3	T	1	1	at_home	other	...	yes	no	5	3	3	1	1	3	2
2	GP	F	15	U	LE3	T	1	1	at_home	other	...	yes	no	4	3	2	2	3	3	6
3	GP	F	15	U	GT3	T	4	2	health	services	...	yes	yes	3	2	2	1	1	5	0
4	GP	F	16	U	GT3	T	3	3	other	other	...	no	no	4	3	2	1	2	5	0

5 rows × 31 columns

As mentioned before, some of these columns are words or phrases, such as **Mjob**, **Fjob**, **internet**, and **romantic**. These columns need to be converted into numbers, which can be done using the `get_dummies` function, which is a Pandas feature, and we need to mention which columns are the ones that we want to turn into numeric form.

In the case of **Mjob**, for example, the function it is going to look at all the different possible answers or the values in that column and it's going to give each value a column name. These columns will receive names such as rename the columns to **Mjob at_home**, **Mjob health**, or **Mjob**. These new columns, for example, the **Mjob at_home** column will have value **1** and the rest will have **0**. This means only one of the new columns generated will have one.

This is know as **one-hot encoding**. The reason this name was given is for example, imagine some wires going into a circuit. Suppose in the circuit there are five wires, and you want use one-hot encoding method, you need to activate only one of these wires while keeping the rest of wires off.

On performing `get_dummies` function on our dataset, You can notice for example **activities_no** and **activities_yes** columns. The originally associated columns that said no had 1 as value under **activies_no** column followed by 0. The same as for **activities_yes** had yes it would have a value 0 followed by 1 for others. This led to creation of many more new columns around 57 in total but this made our dataset full of numeric data. The following screenshot shows the columns **activities_yes** and **activities_no** columns:

```
In [3]:   # use one-hot encoding on categorical columns
          d = pd.get_dummies(d, columns=['sex', 'school', 'address', 'famsize', 'Pstatus', 'Mjob', 'Fjob',
                                         'reason', 'guardian', 'schoolsup', 'famsup', 'paid', 'activities',
                                         'nursery', 'higher', 'internet', 'romantic'])
          d.head()
```

Out[3]:

	age	Medu	Fedu	traveltime	studytime	failures	famrel	freetime	goout	Dalc	...	activities_no	activities_yes	nursery_no
0	18	4	4	2	2	0	4	3	4	1	...	1	0	0
1	17	1	1	1	2	0	5	3	3	1	...	1	0	1
2	15	1	1	1	2	0	4	3	2	2	...	1	0	0
3	15	4	2	1	3	0	3	2	2	1	...	0	1	0
4	16	3	3	1	2	0	4	3	2	1	...	1	0	0

5 rows × 57 columns

Here we need to shuffle the rows and produce a training set with first 500 rows and rest 149 rows for test set and then we just need to get attributes form the training set which means we will get rid of the pass column and save the pass column separately. The same is repeated for the testing set. We will apply the attributes to the entire dataset and save the pass column separately for the entire dataset.

Now we will find how many passed and failed from the entire dataset. This can be done by computing the percentage number of passed and failed which will give us a result of 328 out of 649. This being the pass percentage which is roughly around 50% of the dataset. This constitutes a well-balanced dataset:

```
In [4]:  # shuffle rows
         d = d.sample(frac=1)
         # split training and testing data
         d_train = d[:500]
         d_test = d[500:]

         d_train_att = d_train.drop(['pass'], axis=1)
         d_train_pass = d_train['pass']

         d_test_att = d_test.drop(['pass'], axis=1)
         d_test_pass = d_test['pass']

         d_att = d.drop(['pass'], axis=1)
         d_pass = d['pass']

         # number of passing students in whole dataset:
         import numpy as np
         print("Passing: %d out of %d (%.2f%%)" % (np.sum(d_pass), len(d_pass), 100*float(np.sum(d_pass)) / len(d_pass)))

         Passing: 328 out of 649 (50.54%)
```

Next, we start building the decision tree using the `DecisionTreeClassifier` function from the scikit-learn package, which is a class capable of performing multi-class classification on a dataset. Here we will use the entropy or information gain metric to decide when to split. We will split at a depth of five questions, by using `max_depth=5` as an initial tree depth to get a feel for how the tree is fitting the data:

```
In [5]:  # fit a decision tree
         from sklearn import tree
         t = tree.DecisionTreeClassifier(criterion="entropy", max_depth=5)
         t = t.fit(d_train_att, d_train_pass)
```

To get an overview of our dataset, we need to create a visual representation of the tree. This can be achieved by using one more function of the scikit-learn package: `expoert_graphviz`. The following screenshot shows the representation of the tree in a Jupyter Notebook:

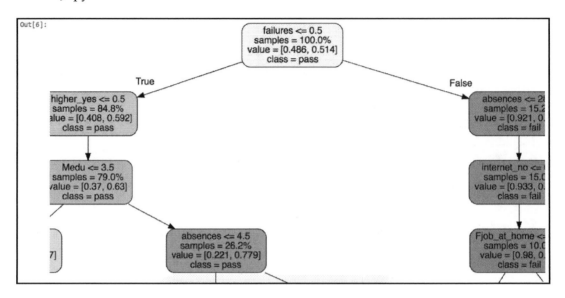

This is for representation, more can be seen on scrolling in Jupyter output

It is pretty much easy to understand the previous representation that the dataset is divided into two parts. Let's try to interpret the tree from the top. In this case if failure is greater than or equal to 0.5, that means it is true and it placed on left-hand side of the tree. Consider tree is always true on left side and false on right side, which means there are no prior failures. In the representation we can see left side of the tree is mostly in blue which means it is predicting a pass even though there are few questions as compared to the failure maximum of 5 questions. The tree is o n right side if failure is less than 0.5, this makes the student fail, which means the first question is false. Prediction is failure if in orange color but as it proceeds further to more questions since we have used `max_depth = 5`.

The following code block shows a method to export the visual representation which by clicking on Export and save to PDF or any format if you want to visualize later:

```
In [7]:  # save tree
         tree.export_graphviz(t, out_file="student-performance.dot", label="all", impurity=False, proportion=True,
                        feature_names=list(d_train_att), class_names=["fail", "pass"],
                        filled=True, rounded=True)
```

Next we check the score of the tree using the testing set that we created earlier:

```
In [8]:  t.score(d_test_att, d_test_pass)

Out[8]:  0.59731543624161076
```

The result we had was approximately 60%. Now let's cross verify the result to be assured that the dataset is trained perfectly:

```
In [9]:  from sklearn.model_selection import cross_val_score
         scores = cross_val_score(t, d_att, d_pass, cv=5)
         # show average score and +/- two standard deviations away (covering 95% of scores)
         print("Accuracy: %0.2f (+/- %0.2f)" % (scores.mean(), scores.std() * 2))

         Accuracy: 0.67 (+/- 0.06)
```

Performing cross-validation on the entire dataset which will split the data on a of 20/80 basis, where 20% is the on testing set and 80% is on the training set. The average result is 67%. This shows that we have a well-balanced dataset. Here we have various choices to make regarding `max_depth`:

```
In [10]:  for max_depth in range(1, 20):
              t = tree.DecisionTreeClassifier(criterion="entropy", max_depth=max_depth)
              scores = cross_val_score(t, d_att, d_pass, cv=5)
              print("Max depth: %d, Accuracy: %0.2f (+/- %0.2f)" % (max_depth, scores.mean(), scores.std() * 2))

          Max depth: 1, Accuracy: 0.64 (+/- 0.05)
          Max depth: 2, Accuracy: 0.69 (+/- 0.08)
          Max depth: 3, Accuracy: 0.69 (+/- 0.09)
          Max depth: 4, Accuracy: 0.66 (+/- 0.10)
          Max depth: 5, Accuracy: 0.67 (+/- 0.06)
          Max depth: 6, Accuracy: 0.64 (+/- 0.08)
          Max depth: 7, Accuracy: 0.67 (+/- 0.02)
          Max depth: 8, Accuracy: 0.67 (+/- 0.07)
          Max depth: 9, Accuracy: 0.67 (+/- 0.06)
          Max depth: 10, Accuracy: 0.63 (+/- 0.12)
          Max depth: 11, Accuracy: 0.65 (+/- 0.07)
          Max depth: 12, Accuracy: 0.63 (+/- 0.07)
          Max depth: 13, Accuracy: 0.63 (+/- 0.07)
          Max depth: 14, Accuracy: 0.63 (+/- 0.08)
          Max depth: 15, Accuracy: 0.64 (+/- 0.06)
          Max depth: 16, Accuracy: 0.62 (+/- 0.05)
          Max depth: 17, Accuracy: 0.64 (+/- 0.09)
          Max depth: 18, Accuracy: 0.63 (+/- 0.08)
          Max depth: 19, Accuracy: 0.63 (+/- 0.06)
```

We use various `max_depth` values from 1 to 20, Considering we make a tree with one question or with 20 questions having depth value of 20 which will give us questions more than 20 which is you will have to go 20 steps down to reach a leaf node. Here we again perform cross- validation and save and print our answer. This will give different accuracy and calculations. On analyzing it was found that on have depth of 2 and 3 the accuracy is the best which was compared accuracy from the average we found earlier.

The following screenshot shows the data that we will be using to the create graph:

```
In [11]:  depth_acc = np.empty((19,3), float)
          i = 0
          for max_depth in range(1, 20):
              t = tree.DecisionTreeClassifier(criterion="entropy", max_depth=max_depth)
              scores = cross_val_score(t, d_att, d_pass, cv=5)
              depth_acc[i,0] = max_depth
              depth_acc[i,1] = scores.mean()
              depth_acc[i,2] = scores.std() * 2
              i += 1

          depth_acc

Out[11]:  array([[  1.      ,  0.63790456,  0.04848398],
                 [  2.      ,  0.68559869,  0.07148267],
                 [  3.      ,  0.68710174,  0.0865951 ],
                 [  4.      ,  0.6669467 ,  0.10726248],
                 [  5.      ,  0.66261518,  0.05307124],
                 [  6.      ,  0.65018859,  0.07040891],
                 [  7.      ,  0.66564494,  0.02029519],
                 [  8.      ,  0.67474598,  0.05984916],
                 [  9.      ,  0.6640118 ,  0.03746891],
                 [ 10.      ,  0.6346137 ,  0.09657669],
                 [ 11.      ,  0.6484015 ,  0.10475147],
                 [ 12.      ,  0.64545485,  0.05529647],
                 [ 13.      ,  0.64544256,  0.08167465],
                 [ 14.      ,  0.6346614 ,  0.07458128],
                 [ 15.      ,  0.63463773,  0.08162646],
                 [ 16.      ,  0.62853141,  0.05926906],
                 [ 17.      ,  0.63622335,  0.05390067],
                 [ 18.      ,  0.62548936,  0.06050112],
                 [ 19.      ,  0.63004547,  0.07022296]])
```

The error bars shown in the following screenshot are the standard deviations in the score, which concludes that a depth of 2 or 3 is ideal for this dataset, and that our assumption of 5 was incorrect:

```
In [12]:   import matplotlib.pyplot as plt
           fig, ax = plt.subplots()
           ax.errorbar(depth_acc[:,0], depth_acc[:,1], yerr=depth_acc[:,2])
           plt.show()
```

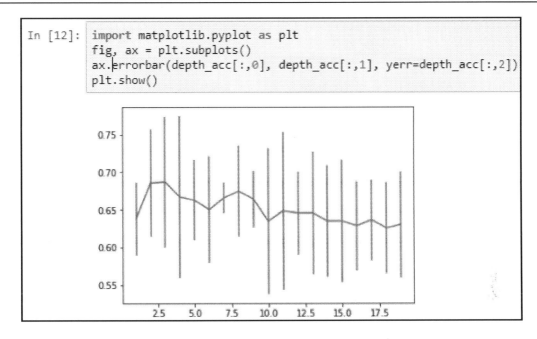

More depth doesn't give any more power, and just having one question, which would be *did you fail previously?*, isn't going to provide you with the same amount of information as two or three questions would.

Our model shows that having more depth does not necessarily help, nor does having a single question of *did you fail previously?* provide us with the same amount of information as two or three questions would give us.

Summary

In this chapter we learned about classification and techniques for evaluation, and learned in depth about decision trees. We also created a model to predict student performance.

In the next chapter, we will learn more about random forests and use machine learning and random forests to predict bird species.

2
Prediction with Random Forests

In this chapter, we're going to look at classification techniques with random forests. We're going to use scikit-learn, just like we did in the previous chapter. We're going to look at examples of predicting bird species from descriptive attributes and then use a confusion matrix on them.

Here's a detailed list of the topics:

- Classification and techniques for evaluation
- Predicting bird species with random forests
- Confusion matrix

Random forests

Random forests are extensions of decision trees and are a kind of ensemble method.

Ensemble methods can achieve high accuracy by building several classifiers and running a each one independently. When a classifier makes a decision, you can make use of the most common and the average decision. If we use the most common method, it is called **voting**.

Here's a diagram depicting the ensemble method:

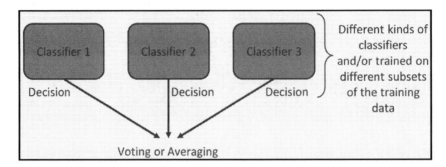

You can think of each classifier as being specialized for a unique perspective on the data. Each classifier may be a different type. For example, you can combine a decision tree and a logistic regression and a neural net, or the classifiers may be the same type but trained on different parts or subsets of the training data.

A random forest is a collection or ensemble of decision trees. Each tree is trained on a random subset of the attributes, as shown in the following diagram:

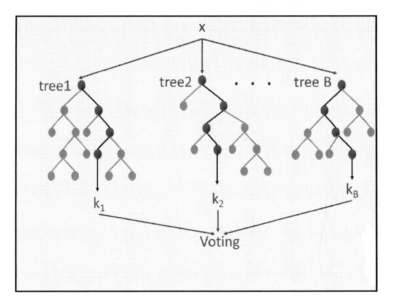

These decision trees are typical decision trees, but there are several of them. The difference, compared with a single decision tree, particularly in a random forest, is that each tree is only allowed to look at some of the attributes, typically a small number relative to the total number of attributes available. Each tree is specialized to just those attributes. These specialized trees are collected and each offers a vote for its prediction. Whichever outcome gets the most votes from the ensemble of specialized trees is the winner. That is the final prediction of the random forest.

Usage of random forest

We should consider using a random forest when there is a sufficient number of attributes to make trees and the accuracy is paramount. When there are fewer trees, the interpretability is difficult compared to a single decision tree. You should avoid using random forests if interpretability is important because if there are too many trees, the models are quite large and can take a lot of memory during training and prediction. Hence, resource-limited environments may not be able to use random forests. The next section will explain the prediction of bird species using random forests.

Predicting bird species with random forests

Here we will be using random forests to predict a bird's species. We will use the Caltech-UC San Diego dataset (`http://www.vision.caltech.edu/visipedia/CUB-200-2011.html`), which contains about 12,000 photos of birds from 200 different species. Here we are not going to look at the pictures because that would need a **convolutional neural network** (**CNN**) and this will be covered in later chapters. CNNs can handle pictures much better than a random forest. Instead, we will be using attributes of the birds such as size, shape, and color.

Here are just some of the species in the dataset:

Some, such as the **American Crow** and the **Fish Crow**, are almost indistinguishable, at least visually. The attributes for each photo, such as color and size, have actually been labeled by humans. Caltech and UCSD used human workers on Amazon's Mechanical Turk to label the dataset. Researchers often use Mechanical Turk, which is a website service in which a person gets paid a tiny amount of money for each photo they label to improve the dataset using human insight rather than machine predictions.

 If you have your own dataset that needs lots of human-provided labels, you might consider spending some money on Mechanical Turk to complete that task.

Here's an example of a single photo and its labels:

Attribute Labels (User Responses)

Has_Bill_Shape: Cone (definitely, 21.5210sec)

Has_Wing_Color: Rufous Red (guessing, 4.7140sec)

Has_Upperparts_Color: Rufous Red (guessing, 25.8140sec)

Has_Underparts_Color: Red (definitely, 7.7670sec)

Has_Breast_Pattern: Solid (definitely, 4.7430sec)

Has_Back_Color: Rufous Red (guessing, 9.3730sec)

Has_Tail_Shape: Notched Tail (definitely, 25.2200sec)

Has_Upper_Tail: Color_Rufous Color_Red (guessing, 4.6720sec)

Has_Head_Pattern: Plain (definitely, 13.6300sec)

Has_Breast_Color: Red (definitely, 5.1320sec)

Has_Throat_Color: Red (definitely, 2.9700sec)

Has_Eye_Color: Black (definitely, 3.2070sec)

Has_Bill_Length: Shorter than Head (definitely, 5.2780sec)

Has_Forehead_Color: Red (definitely, 4.5800sec)

Has_Under_Tail_Color: Rufous Red (guessing, 6.0650sec)

Has_Nape_Color: Red (definitely, 3.6060sec)

Has_Belly_Color: Red (definitely, 4.0580sec)

Has_Wing_Shape: Rounded–Wings (probably, 20.5980sec)

Has_Size: Very Small (3 – 5 in) (probably, 28.1390sec)

Has_Shape: Perching-like (definitely, 27.8350sec)

Has_Back_Pattern: (not visible, 5.1130sec)

Has_Tail_Pattern: (not visible, 6.6540sec)

Has_Belly_Pattern: Solid (definitely, 5.1880sec)

Has_Primary_Color: Rufous Red (definitely, 8.7730sec)

Has_Leg_Color: Grey (definitely, 7.7810sec)

Has_Bill_Color: Brown Buff (definitely, 15.6450sec)

Has_Crown_Color: Red (definitely, 21.9820sec)

Has_Wing_Pattern: (not visible, 6.7080sec)

http://www.vision.caltech.edu/visipedia-data/CUB-200-2011/browse/Summer_Tanager.html

We can see that the Summer Tanager is marked as having a red throat, a solid belly pattern, a perching-like shape, and so on. The dataset includes information about how long it took each person to decide on the labels and how confident the person is with their decisions, but we're not going to use that information.

The data is split into several files. We'll discuss those files before jumping into the code:

Class ids/names (classes.txt)	Image ids/file names (images.txt)	Image ids/class ids (image_class_labels.txt)
1 001.Black_footed_Albatross	1 001.Black_footed_Albatross/Black_Footed_Albatross_0046_18.jpg	1 1
2 002.Laysan_Albatross	2 001.Black_footed_Albatross/Black_Footed_Albatross_0009_34.jpg	2 1
3 003.Sooty_Albatross	3 001.Black_footed_Albatross/Black_Footed_Albatross_0002_55.jpg	3 1
4 004.Groove_billed_Ani	4 001.Black_footed_Albatross/Black_Footed_Albatross_0074_59.jpg	4 1
5 005.Crested_Auklet	5 001.Black_footed_Albatross/Black_Footed_Albatross_0014_89.jpg	5 1
6 006.Least_Auklet	6 001.Black_footed_Albatross/Black_Footed_Albatross_0085_92.jpg	6 1
7 007.Parakeet_Auklet	7 001.Black_footed_Albatross/Black_Footed_Albatross_0031_100.jpg	7 1
8 008.Rhinoceros_Auklet	8 001.Black_footed_Albatross/Black_Footed_Albatross_0051_796103.jpg	8 1
9 009.Brewer_Blackbird	9 001.Black_footed_Albatross/Black_Footed_Albatross_0010_796097.jpg	9 1
10 010.Red_winged_Blackbird	10 001.Black_footed_Albatross/Black_Footed_Albatross_0025_796057.jpg	10 1

The `classes.txt` file shows class IDs with the bird species names. The `images.txt` file shows image IDs and filenames. The species for each photo is given in the `image_class_labels.txt` file, which connects the class IDs with the image IDs.

The `attributes.txt` file gives the name of each attribute, which ultimately is not going to be that important to us. We're only going to need the attribute IDs:

```
Attribute ids/names
(attributes.txt)

1  has_bill_shape::curved_(up_or_down)
2  has_bill_shape::dagger
3  has_bill_shape::hooked
4  has_bill_shape::needle
5  has_bill_shape::hooked_seabird
6  has_bill_shape::spatulate
7  has_bill_shape::all-purpose
8  has_bill_shape::cone
9  has_bill_shape::specialized
10 has_wing_color::blue
11 has_wing_color::brown
12 has_wing_color::iridescent
13 has_wing_color::purple
14 has_wing_color::rufous
```

Finally, the most important file is `image_attribute_labels.txt`:

```
            Image-id, attribute-id, present/absent (1/0)
            (image_attribute_labels.txt)

              1  1  0 3 27.7080
              1  2  0 3 27.7080
              1  3  0 3 27.7080
image id      1  4  0 3 27.7080
              1  5  1 3 27.7080
              1  6  0 3 27.7080
attribute id  1  7  0 3 27.7080
              1  8  0 3 27.7080
              1  9  0 3 27.7080
              1 10  0 1 1.7040
              1 11  0 1 1.7040
              1 12  0 1 1.7040
1=present,    1 13  0 1 1.7040
0=absent      1 14  0 1 1.7040
              1 15  0 1 1.7040
              1 16  0 1 1.7040
              1 17  0 1 1.7040
```

It connects each image with its attributes in a binary value that's either present or absent for that attribute. Users on Mechanical Turk produced each row in this file.

Now, let's look at the code:

```
In [44]: import pandas as pd

         # some lines have too many fields (?), so skip bad lines
         imgatt = pd.read_csv("data/CUB_200_2011/attributes/image_attribute_labels.txt",
                         sep='\s+', header=None, error_bad_lines=False, warn_bad_lines=False,
                         usecols=[0,1,2], names=['imgid', 'attid', 'present'])

         # description from dataset README:
         #
         # The set of attribute labels as perceived by MTurkers for each image
         # is contained in the file attributes/image_attribute_labels.txt, with
         # each line corresponding to one image/attribute/worker triplet:
         #
         # <image_id> <attribute_id> <is_present> <certainty_id> <time>
         #
         # where <image_id>, <attribute_id>, <certainty_id> correspond to the IDs
         # in images.txt, attributes/attributes.txt, and attributes/certainties.txt
         # respectively.  <is_present> is 0 or 1 (1 denotes that the attribute is
         # present).  <time> denotes the time spent by the MTurker in seconds.
```

We will first load the CSV file with all the image attribute labels.

Here are few things that need to be noted:

- Space separation for all the values
- No header column or row
- Ignore the messages or warnings, such as `error_bad_lines= False` and `warn_bad_lines= False`
- Use columns 0, 1, and 2, which have the image ID, the attribute ID, and the present or non-present value

You don't need to worry about the attributes and the time taken to select them.

Here, at the top of that dataset:

```
In [45]:  imgatt.head()
```

Out[45]:

	imgid	attid	present
0	1	1	0
1	1	2	0
2	1	3	0
3	1	4	0
4	1	5	1

Image ID number 1 does not have attributes 1, 2, 3, or 4, but it does have attribute 5.

The shape will tell us how many rows and columns we have:

```
In [46]:  imgatt.shape
```

Out[46]: (3677856, 3)

It has 3.7 million rows and three columns. This is not the actual formula that you want. You want attributes to be the columns, not rows.

```
In [47]:  # need to reorganize imgatt to have one row per imgid, and 312 columns (one column per attribute),
          # with 1/0 in each cell representing if that imgid has that attribute or not

          imgatt2 = imgatt.pivot(index='imgid', columns='attid', values='present')
```

Therefore, we have to use pivot, just like Excel has a pivot method:

1. Pivot on the image ID and make one row for each image ID. There will be only one row for image number one.
2. Turn the attributes into distinct columns, and the values will be ones or twos.

We can now see that each image ID is just one row and each attribute is its own column, and we have the ones and the twos:

```
In [48]:  imgatt2.head()
```

attid	1	2	3	4	5	6	7	8	9	10	...	303	304	305	306	307	308	309	310	311	312
imgid																					
1	0	0	0	0	1	0	0	0	0	0	...	0	0	0	0	0	1	0	0	0	0
2	0	0	0	0	0	0	0	0	0	0	...	0	0	0	0	0	0	0	0	0	0
3	0	0	0	0	1	0	0	0	0	0	...	0	0	0	0	0	1	0	0	1	0
4	0	0	0	0	1	0	0	0	0	0	...	0	0	0	1	0	0	1	0	0	0
5	0	0	0	0	1	0	0	0	0	0	...	0	0	1	0	0	0	0	0	0	0

5 rows × 312 columns

Let's feed this data into a random forest. In the previous example, we have 312 columns and 312 attributes, which is ultimately about 12,000 images or 12,000 different examples of birds:

```
In [49]:  imgatt2.shape
Out[49]:  (11788, 312)
```

Now, we need to load the answers, such as whether it's a bird and which species it is. Since it is an image class labels file, the separators are spaces. There is no header row and the two columns are imgid and label. We will be using set_index('imgid') to have the same result produced by imgatt2.head(), where the rows are identified by the image ID:

```
In [50]:  # now we need to load the image true classes

          imglabels = pd.read_csv("data/CUB_200_2011/image_class_labels.txt",
                        sep=' ', header=None, names=['imgid', 'label'])

          imglabels = imglabels.set_index('imgid')

          # description from dataset README:
          #
          # The ground truth class labels (bird species labels) for each image are contained
          # in the file image_class_labels.txt, with each line corresponding to one image:
          #
          # <image_id> <class_id>
          #
          # where <image_id> and <class_id> correspond to the IDs in images.txt and classes.txt,
          # respectively.
```

Here's what it looks like:

```
In [51]:  imglabels.head()

Out[51]:                    label

               imgid

                   1          1

                   2          1

                   3          1

                   4          1

                   5          1
```

The `imgid` column has 1, 2, 3, 4, and 5, all are labeled as 1. They're all albatrossed at the top of the file. As seen, there are about 12,000 rows, which is perfect:

```
In [52]:  imglabels.shape

Out[52]:  (11788, 1)
```

This is the same number as the attributes data. We will be using join.

In the join, we will use the index on the image ID to join the two data frames. Effectively, what we're going to get is that the label is stuck on as the last column.

We will be now shuffling and then be splitting off the attributes. In other words, we want to drop the label from the label. So, here are the attributes, with the first 312 columns and the last column being a label:

```
In [53]:  # now we need to attach the labels to the attribute data set,
          # and shuffle; then we'll separate a test set from a training set

          df = imgatt2.join(imglabels)
          df = df.sample(frac=1)
```

```
In [54]:  df_att = df.iloc[:, :312]
          df_label = df.iloc[:, 312:]
```

```
In [55]:  df_att.head()
```

Out[55]:

	1	2	3	4	5	6	7	8	9	10	...	303	304	305	306	307	308	309	310	311	312
imgid																					
527	0	0	0	0	0	0	1	0	0	0	...	0	0	1	0	0	0	0	0	0	1
1532	1	0	0	0	0	0	0	0	0	0	...	0	0	0	0	0	0	0	1	0	0
9137	0	0	0	0	0	0	1	0	0	0	...	0	0	1	0	0	0	0	0	0	1
487	0	1	0	0	0	0	0	0	0	0	...	0	0	1	0	0	0	0	0	0	1
2444	0	0	0	0	0	0	0	1	0	0	...	0	0	0	0	0	0	0	0	0	1

5 rows × 312 columns

After shuffling, we have the first row as image 527, the second row as image 1532, and so forth. The attributes in the label data are in agreement. On the first row, it's image 527, which is the number 10. You will not know which bird it is, but it's of the kind, and these are its attributes. But it is finally in the right form. We need to do a training test split.

There were 12,000 rows, so let's take the first 8,000 and call them training, and the call rest of them testing (4,000). We'll get the answers using `RandomForestClassifier`:

```
In [57]:  df_train_att = df_att[:8000]
          df_train_label = df_label[:8000]
          df_test_att = df_att[8000:]
          df_test_label = df_label[8000:]

          df_train_label = df_train_label['label']
          df_test_label = df_test_label['label']
```

```
In [58]:  from sklearn.ensemble import RandomForestClassifier
          clf = RandomForestClassifier(max_features=50, random_state=0, n_estimators=100)
```

Max features show the number of different columns each tree can look at.

For an instance, if we say something like, *look at two attributes*, that's probably not enough to actually figure out which bird it is. Some birds are unique, so you might need a lot more attributes. Later if we say `max_features=50` and the number of estimators denote the number of trees created. The fit actually builds it.

```
In [59]: clf.fit(df_train_att, df_train_label)

Out[59]: RandomForestClassifier(bootstrap=True, class_weight=None, criterion='gini',
                     max_depth=None, max_features=50, max_leaf_nodes=None,
                     min_impurity_decrease=0.0, min_impurity_split=None,
                     min_samples_leaf=1, min_samples_split=2,
                     min_weight_fraction_leaf=0.0, n_estimators=100, n_jobs=1,
                     oob_score=False, random_state=0, verbose=0, warm_start=False)
```

Let's predict a few cases. Let's use attributes from the first five rows of the training set, which will predict species 10, 28, 156, 10, and 43. After testing, we get 44% accuracy:

```
In [60]: print clf.predict(df_train_att.head())

         [ 10  28 156  10  43]

In [61]: clf.score(df_test_att, df_test_label)

Out[61]: 0.44297782470960928
```

Even 44% accuracy is not the best result. There are 200 species, so having 0.5% accuracy is much better than randomly guessing.

Making a confusion matrix for the data

Let's make a confusion matrix to see which birds the dataset confuses. The `confusion_matrix` function from scikit-learn will produce the matrix, but it's a pretty big matrix:

```
In [62]:  from sklearn.metrics import confusion_matrix
          pred_labels = clf.predict(df_test_att)
          cm = confusion_matrix(df_test_label, pred_labels)

In [63]:  cm

Out[63]:  array([[ 5,  1,  6, ...,  0,  1,  0],
                 [ 0, 12,  0, ...,  0,  0,  0],
                 [ 0,  0,  8, ...,  0,  0,  0],
                 ...,
                 [ 0,  0,  0, ...,  6,  0,  0],
                 [ 0,  0,  0, ...,  0, 11,  0],
                 [ 0,  0,  0, ...,  0,  0, 13]]])
```

Two hundred by two hundred is not easy to understand in a numeric form like this.

Here's some code from the scikit-learn documentation that allows us to plot the matrix and the color in the matrix:

```
In [64]:  # from http://scikit-learn.org/stable/auto_examples/model_selection/plot_confusion_matrix.html
          import matplotlib.pyplot as plt
          import itertools
          def plot_confusion_matrix(cm, classes,
                                    normalize=False,
                                    title='Confusion matrix',
                                    cmap=plt.cm.Blues):
              """
              This function prints and plots the confusion matrix.
              Normalization can be applied by setting `normalize=True`.
              """
              if normalize:
                  cm = cm.astype('float') / cm.sum(axis=1)[:, np.newaxis]
                  print("Normalized confusion matrix")
              else:
                  print('Confusion matrix, without normalization')

              print(cm)

              plt.imshow(cm, interpolation='nearest', cmap=cmap)
              plt.title(title)
              #plt.colorbar()
              tick_marks = np.arange(len(classes))
              plt.xticks(tick_marks, classes, rotation=90)
              plt.yticks(tick_marks, classes)

              fmt = '.2f' if normalize else 'd'
              thresh = cm.max() / 2.
              #for i, j in itertools.product(range(cm.shape[0]), range(cm.shape[1])):
              #    plt.text(j, i, format(cm[i, j], fmt),
              #             horizontalalignment="center",
              #             color="white" if cm[i, j] > thresh else "black")

              plt.tight_layout()
              plt.ylabel('True label')
              plt.xlabel('Predicted label')
```

We will need the actual names of the birds on the matrix so that we know the species that are being confused for each other. So, let's load the classes file:

```
In [65]:  birds = pd.read_csv("data/CUB_200_2011/classes.txt",
                    sep='\s+', header=None, usecols=[1], names=['birdname'])
          birds = birds['birdname']
          birds

Out[65]: 0                 001.Black_footed_Albatross
         1                     002.Laysan_Albatross
         2                      003.Sooty_Albatross
         3                     004.Groove_billed_Ani
         4                       005.Crested_Auklet
         5                         006.Least_Auklet
         6                      007.Parakeet_Auklet
         7                    008.Rhinoceros_Auklet
         8                      009.Brewer_Blackbird
         9                 010.Red_winged_Blackbird
         10                     011.Rusty_Blackbird
         11           012.Yellow_headed_Blackbird
         12                             013.Bobolink
         13                     014.Indigo_Bunting
         14                     015.Lazuli_Bunting
         15                   016.Painted_Bunting
         16                           017.Cardinal
         17                   018.Spotted_Catbird
         18                       019.Gray_Catbird
         19             020.Yellow_breasted_Chat
         20                     021.Eastern_Towhee
         21                 022.Chuck_will_Widow
         22                     023.Brandt_Cormorant
         23             024.Red_faced_Cormorant
         24                 025.Pelagic_Cormorant
         25                   026.Bronzed_Cowbird
         26                     027.Shiny_Cowbird
         27                     028.Brown_Creeper
         28                   029.American_Crow
         29                         030.Fish_Crow
```

Plot the matrix. This is the confusion matrix for this dataset:

```
In [66]:  import numpy as np
          np.set_printoptions(precision=2)
          plt.figure(figsize=(60,60), dpi=300)
          plot_confusion_matrix(cm, classes=birds, normalize=True)
          plt.show()

          Normalized confusion matrix
          [[ 0.22  0.04  0.26 ...,  0.    0.04  0.   ]
           [ 0.    0.57  0.    ...,  0.    0.    0.   ]
           [ 0.    0.    0.44 ...,  0.    0.    0.   ]
           ...,
           [ 0.    0.    0.    ...,  0.25  0.    0.   ]
           [ 0.    0.    0.    ...,  0.    0.55  0.   ]
           [ 0.    0.    0.    ...,  0.    0.    0.76]]
```

The output looks like the following:

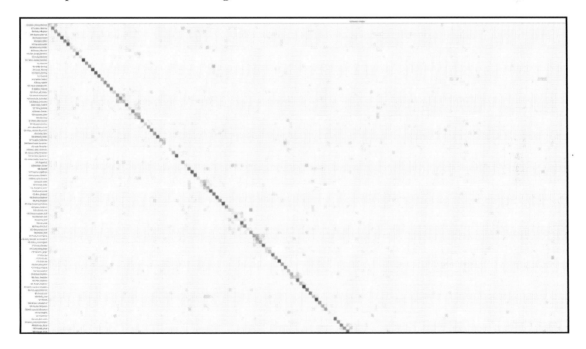

The output is unreadable because there are 200 rows and columns. But if we open it separately and then start zooming in, on the *y* axis you will see the actual birds, and on the *x* axis, you will see the predicted birds:

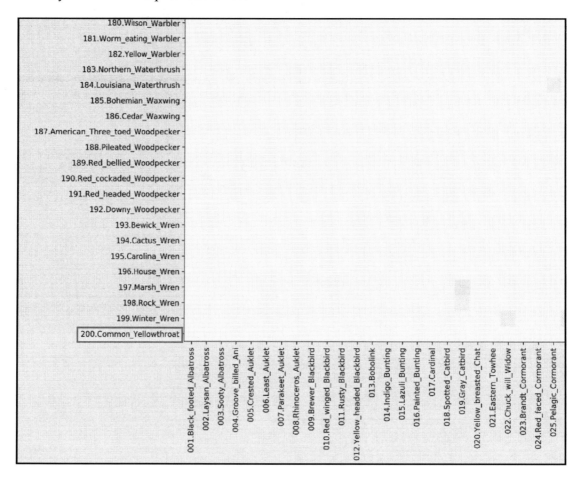

For example, the common yellow throat is the true one. Looking at the following graph, we can see that the common yellow throat is confused with the black-footed albatross. When we zoom out, we will see the confusion:

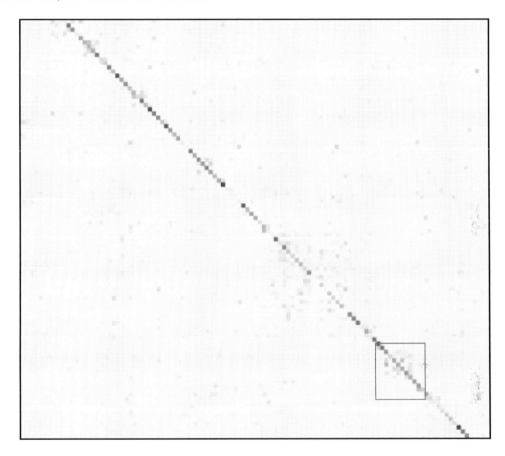

It's like a square of confusion that was there between the common yellow throat and the black-footed albatross. Some features are terns, such as the arctic tern, black tern, Caspian tern, and the common tern. Terns are apparently easy to confuse because they look similar.

This set is a little bit confused too:

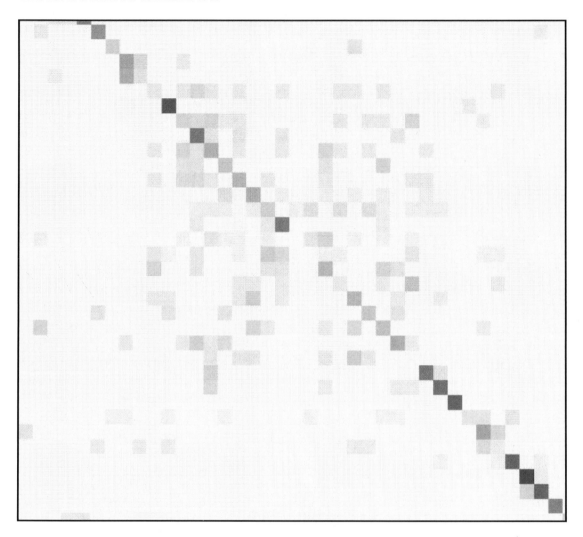

This is the set regarding sparrows. The confusion matrix tells us the things that we expect, that is, birds that look similar are confused with each other. There are little squares of confusion, as seen in the previous screenshot.

For the most part, you don't want to confuse an albatross with a common yellow throat because this means that the dataset doesn't know with what it's doing.

Since the bird's names are sorted, lesser is the square of confusion. Let's compare this with the simple decision tree:

```
In [67]:  from sklearn import tree
          clftree = tree.DecisionTreeClassifier()
          clftree.fit(df_train_att, df_train_label)
          clftree.score(df_test_att, df_test_label)

Out[67]:  0.26953537486800422
```

Here, the accuracy is 27%, which is less than the previous 44% accuracy. Therefore, the decision tree is worse. If we use a **Support Vector Machine (SVM)**, which is the neural network approach, the output is 29%:

```
In [68]:  from sklearn import svm
          clfsvm = svm.SVC()
          clfsvm.fit(df_train_att, df_train_label)
          clfsvm.score(df_test_att, df_test_label)

Out[68]:  0.28616684266103487
```

The random forest is still better.

Let's perform cross-validation to make sure that we split the training test in different ways. The output is still 44% for the random forest, 25% for our decision tree, and 27% for SVM, as shown in the following screenshot:

```
In [69]:  from sklearn.model_selection import cross_val_score
          scores = cross_val_score(clf, df_train_att, df_train_label, cv=5)
          # show average score and +/- two standard deviations away (covering 95% of scores)
          print("Accuracy: %0.2f (+/- %0.2f)" % (scores.mean(), scores.std() * 2))

          Accuracy: 0.44 (+/- 0.02)

In [70]:  scorestree = cross_val_score(clftree, df_train_att, df_train_label, cv=5)
          print("Accuracy: %0.2f (+/- %0.2f)" % (scorestree.mean(), scorestree.std() * 2))

          Accuracy: 0.25 (+/- 0.02)

In [71]:  scoressvm = cross_val_score(clfsvm, df_train_att, df_train_label, cv=5)
          print("Accuracy: %0.2f (+/- %0.2f)" % (scoressvm.mean(), scoressvm.std() * 2))

          Accuracy: 0.27 (+/- 0.01)
```

The best results are reflected through random forests since we had some options and questions with random forests.

For example, how many different questions can each tree ask? How many attributes does it look at, and how many trees are there? Well, there are a lot of parameters to look through, so let's just make a loop and try them all:

```
In [72]: max_features_opts = range(5, 50, 5)
         n_estimators_opts = range(10, 200, 20)
         rf_params = np.empty((len(max_features_opts)*len(n_estimators_opts),4), float)
         i = 0
         for max_features in max_features_opts:
             for n_estimators in n_estimators_opts:
                 clf = RandomForestClassifier(max_features=max_features, n_estimators=n_estimators)
                 scores = cross_val_score(clf, df_train_att, df_train_label, cv=5)
                 rf_params[i,0] = max_features
                 rf_params[i,1] = n_estimators
                 rf_params[i,2] = scores.mean()
                 rf_params[i,3] = scores.std() * 2
                 i += 1
                 print("Max features: %d, num estimators: %d, accuracy: %0.2f (+/- %0.2f)" % \
                     (max_features, n_estimators, scores.mean(), scores.std() * 2))
```
```
Max features: 5, num estimators: 10, accuracy: 0.26 (+/- 0.03)
Max features: 5, num estimators: 30, accuracy: 0.35 (+/- 0.02)
Max features: 5, num estimators: 50, accuracy: 0.39 (+/- 0.03)
Max features: 5, num estimators: 70, accuracy: 0.40 (+/- 0.04)
Max features: 5, num estimators: 90, accuracy: 0.42 (+/- 0.02)
Max features: 5, num estimators: 110, accuracy: 0.43 (+/- 0.02)
Max features: 5, num estimators: 130, accuracy: 0.44 (+/- 0.02)
Max features: 5, num estimators: 150, accuracy: 0.44 (+/- 0.03)
Max features: 5, num estimators: 170, accuracy: 0.45 (+/- 0.03)
Max features: 5, num estimators: 190, accuracy: 0.44 (+/- 0.02)
Max features: 10, num estimators: 10, accuracy: 0.29 (+/- 0.03)
Max features: 10, num estimators: 30, accuracy: 0.38 (+/- 0.03)
Max features: 10, num estimators: 50, accuracy: 0.40 (+/- 0.03)
Max features: 10, num estimators: 70, accuracy: 0.42 (+/- 0.02)
Max features: 10, num estimators: 90, accuracy: 0.43 (+/- 0.02)
Max features: 10, num estimators: 110, accuracy: 0.44 (+/- 0.03)
Max features: 10, num estimators: 130, accuracy: 0.44 (+/- 0.03)
Max features: 10, num estimators: 150, accuracy: 0.45 (+/- 0.02)
Max features: 10, num estimators: 170, accuracy: 0.45 (+/- 0.03)
Max features: 10, num estimators: 190, accuracy: 0.45 (+/- 0.03)
Max features: 15, num estimators: 10, accuracy: 0.30 (+/- 0.02)
Max features: 15, num estimators: 30, accuracy: 0.39 (+/- 0.02)
Max features: 15, num estimators: 50, accuracy: 0.42 (+/- 0.02)
Max features: 15, num estimators: 70, accuracy: 0.42 (+/- 0.02)
Max features: 15, num estimators: 90, accuracy: 0.44 (+/- 0.03)
Max features: 15, num estimators: 110, accuracy: 0.44 (+/- 0.03)
Max features: 15, num estimators: 130, accuracy: 0.44 (+/- 0.02)
Max features: 15, num estimators: 150, accuracy: 0.45 (+/- 0.03)
Max features: 15, num estimators: 170, accuracy: 0.45 (+/- 0.03)
```

These are all the accuracies, but it would be better to visualize this in a graph, as shown here:

```
In [90]:  import matplotlib.pyplot as plt
          from mpl_toolkits.mplot3d import Axes3D
          from matplotlib import cm
          fig = plt.figure()
          fig.clf()
          ax = fig.gca(projection='3d')
          x = rf_params[:,0]
          y = rf_params[:,1]
          z = rf_params[:,2]
          ax.scatter(x, y, z)
          ax.set_zlim(0.2, 0.5)
          ax.set_xlabel('Max features')
          ax.set_ylabel('Num estimators')
          ax.set_zlabel('Avg accuracy')
          plt.show()
```

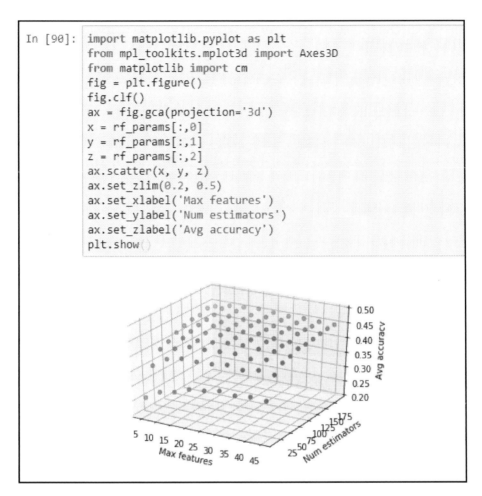

We can see that increasing the number of trees produces a better outcome. Also, increasing the number of features produces better outcomes if you are able to see more features, but ultimately, if you're at about 20 to 30 features and you have about 75 to 100 trees, that's about as good as you're going to get an accuracy of 45%.

Summary

In this chapter, we learned about random forests and classify bird species . Later, we discussed the confusion matrix and different graphs that gave us output based on random trees, decision trees, and SVM.

In the next chapter, we'll go look at comment classification using bag-of-words models and Word2Vec models.

3

Applications for Comment Classification

In this chapter, we'll overview the bag-of-words model for text classification. We will look at predicting YouTube comment spam with the bag-of-words and the random forest techniques. Then we'll look at the Word2Vec models and prediction of positive and negative reviews with the Word2Vec approach and the k-nearest neighbor classifier.

In this chapter, we will particularly focus on text and words and classify internet comments as spam or not spam or to identify internet reviews as positive or negative. We will also have an overview for bag of words for text classification and prediction model to predict YouTube comments are spam or not using bag of words and random forest techniques. We will also look at Word2Vec models an k-nearest neighbor classifier.

But, before we start, we'll answer the following question: *what makes text classification an interesting problem?*

Text classification

To find the answer to our question, we will consider the famous iris flower dataset as an example dataset. The following image is of iris versicolor species. To identify the species, we need some more information other than just an image of the species, such as the flower's **Petal length**, **Petal width**, **Sepal length**, and **Sepal width** would help us identify the image better:

The dataset not only contains examples of versicolor but also contains examples of setosa and virginica as well. Every example in the dataset contains these four measurements. The dataset contains around 150 examples, with 50 examples of each species. We can use a decision tree or any other model to predict the species of a new flower, if provided with the same four measurements. As we know same species will have almost similar measurements. Since similarity has different definition all together but here we consider similarity as the closeness on a graph, if we consider each point is a flower. The following graph is a comparison between sepal width versus petal width:

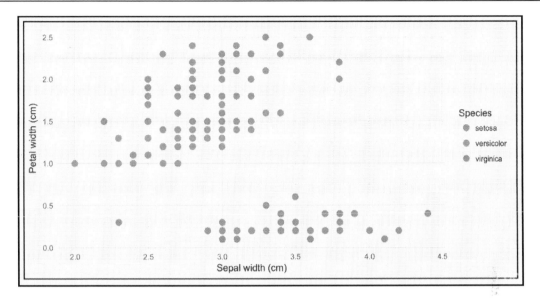

If we had no way of measuring similarity, if, say, every flower had different measurements, then there'd be no way to use machine learning to build a classifier.

As we are aware of the fact that flowers of same species have same measurement and that helps us to distinguish different species. Consider what if every flower had different measurement, it would of no use to build classifier using machine learning to identify images of species.

Machine learning techniques

Before to that we considered images, let's now consider text. For example, consider the following sentences and try to find what makes the first pair of phrases similar to the second pair:

But what makes these phrases similar	And these dissimilar?
Please subscribe to my channel and I will subscribe back xx	The funny thing is that this song was made in 2009 but it took two years to get to America
Guys please subscribe me to help my channel grow please guys	Check my channel please! and listen to the best music ever :P

I hope you got the answer to that question, otherwise we will not be able to build a decision tree, a random forest or anything else to predict the model. To answer the question, notice that the top pair of phrases are similar as they contain some words in common, such as **subscribe** and **channel**, while the second pair of sentences have fewer words in common, such as **to** and **the**. Consider the each phrase representing vector of numbers in a way that the top pair is similar to the numbers in the second pair. Only then we will be able to use random forest or another technique for classification, in this case, to detect YouTube comment spam. To achieve this, we need to use the bag-of-words model.

Bag of words

The bag-of-words model does exactly we want that is to convert the phrases or sentences and counts the number of times a similar word appears. In the world of computer science, a bag refers to a data structure that keeps track of objects like an array or list does, but in such cases the order does not matter and if an object appears more than once, we just keep track of the count rather we keep repeating them.

For example, consider the first phrase from the previous diagram, it has a bag of words that contents words such as **channel**, with one occurrence, **plz**, with one occurrence, **subscribe**, two occurrences, and so on. Then, we would collect all these counts in a vector, where one vector per phrase or sentence or document, depending on what you are working with. Again, the order in which the words appeared originally doesn't matter.

The vector that we created can also be used to sort data alphabetically, but it needs to be done consistently for all the different phrases. However, we still have the same problem. Each phrase has a vector with different columns, because each phrase has different words and a different number of columns, as shown in the following two tables:

○ Example one –

and	back	channel	i	my	plz	subscribe	to	xx
1	1	1	1	1	1	2	1	1

○ Example two –

channel	grow	guys	help	me	my	please	subscribe	to
1	1	2	1	1	1	2	1	1

If we make a larger vector with all the unique words across both phrases, we get a proper matrix representation. With each row representing a different phrase, notice the use of **0** to indicate that a phrase doesn't have a word:

	and	back	channel	grow	guys	help	i	me	my	please	plz	subscribe	to	xx
Example one	1	1	1	0	0	0	1	0	1	0	1	2	1	1
Example two	0	0	1	1	2	1	0	1	1	1	0	1	1	0

If you want to have a bag of words with lots of phrases, documents, or we would need to collect all the unique words that occur across all the examples and create a huge matrix, N x M, where N is the number of examples and M is the number of occurrences. We could easily have thousands of dimensions compared in a four-dimensional model for the iris dataset. The bag of words matrix is likely to be sparse, meaning mostly zeros, since most phrases don't have most words.

Before we start building our bag of words model, we need to take care of a few things, such as the following:

- Lowercase every word
- Drop punctuation
- Drop very common words (stop words)
- Remove plurals (for example, bunnies => bunny)
- Perform lemmatization (for example, reader => read, reading = read)
- Use n-grams, such as bigrams (two-word pairs) or trigrams
- Keep only frequent words (for example, must appear in >10 examples)
- Keep only the most frequent M words (for example, keep only 1,000)
- Record binary counts (*1* = present, *0* = absent) rather than true counts

There are many other combinations for best practice, and finding the best that suits the particular data needs some research.

The problem that we face with long documents is that they will have higher word counts generally, but we may still want to consider long documents about some topic to be considered, similar to a short document about the same topic, even though the word counts will differ significantly.

Furthermore, if we still wanted to reduce very common words and highlight the rare ones, what we would need to do is record the relative importance of each word rather than its raw count. This is known as **term frequency inverse document frequency (TF-IDF)**, which measures how common a word or term is in the document.

We use logarithms to ensure that long documents with many words are very similar to short documents with similar words. TF-IDF has two components that multiply, that is when TF is high, the result is high but IDF measures how common the word is among all the documents and that will affect the common words. So, a word that is common in other documents will have a low score, regardless of how many times it appeared.

If a document has a low score which means the word appeared rarely and if the score is high it means the word appears frequently in the document. But if the word is quite common in all the documents then it becomes irrelevant to score on this document. It is anyhow considered to have low score. This shows that the formula for TF-IDF exhibits in a way we want our model to be. The following graph explains our theory:

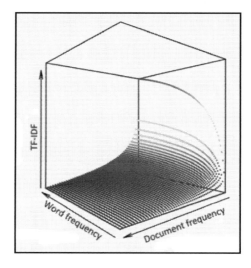

We will be using the bag-of-words method to detect whether YouTube comments are spam or .

Detecting YouTube comment spam

In this section, we're going to look at a technique for detecting YouTube comment spam using bags of words and random forests. The dataset is pretty straightforward. We'll use a dataset that has about 2,000 comments from popular YouTube videos (https://archive.ics.uci.edu/ml/datasets/YouTube+Spam+Collection). The dataset is formatted in a way where each row has a comment followed by a value marked as 1 or 0 for spam or not spam.

First, we will import a single dataset. This dataset is actually split into four different files. Our set of comments comes from the PSY-Gangnam Style video:

```
In [1]:  import pandas as pd
         d = pd.read_csv("D:/Chapter04/Youtube01-Psy.csv")
```

Then we will print a few comments as follows:

```
In [2]:  d.tail()
Out[2]:
```

	COMMENT_ID	DATE	CONTENT	CLASS
345	z13th1q4yzihf1bll23qxzpjeujterydj	2014-11-14T13:27:52	How can this have 2 billion views when there's...	0
346	z13fcn1wfpb5e51xe04chdxakpzgchyaxzo0k	2014-11-14T13:28:08	I don't now why I'm watching this in 2014	0
347	z130zd5b3titudkoe04ccbeohojxuzppvbg	2015-05-23T13:04:32	subscribe to me for call of duty vids and give...	1
348	z12he50arvrkivl5u04cctawgxzkjfsjcc4	2015-06-05T14:14:48	hi guys please my android photo editor downloa...	1
349	z13vhvu54u3ewpp5h04ccb4zuoardrmjlyk0k	2015-06-05T18:05:16	The first billion viewed this because they tho...	0

Here we are able to see that there are more than two columns, but we will only require the content and the class columns. The content column contains the comments and the class column contains the values 1 or 0 for spam or not spam. For example, notice that the first two comments are marked as not spam, but then the comment **subscribe to me for call of duty vids** is spam and **hi guys please my android photo editor download yada yada** is spam as well. Before we start sorting comments, let's look at the count of how many rows in the dataset are spam and how many are not spam. The result we acquired is 175 and 175 respectively, which sums up to 350 rows overall in this file:

```
In [3]:  len(d.query('CLASS == 1'))
Out[3]:  175

In [4]:  len(d.query('CLASS == 0'))
Out[4]:  175

In [5]:  len(d)
Out[5]:  350
```

In scikit-learn, the bag of words technique is actually called `CountVectorizer`, which means counting how many times each word appears and puts them into a vector. To create a vector, we need to make an object for `CountVectorizer`, and then perform the fit and transform simultaneously:

```
In [6]: from sklearn.feature_extraction.text import CountVectorizer
        vectorizer = CountVectorizer()

In [7]: dvec = vectorizer.fit_transform(d['CONTENT'])
```

This performed in two different steps. First comes the fit step, where it discovers which words are present in the dataset, and second is the transform step, which gives you the bag of words matrix for those phrases. The result obtained in that matrix is 350 rows by 1,418 columns:

```
In [7]: dvec = vectorizer.fit_transform(d['CONTENT'])

In [8]: dvec

Out[8]: <350x1418 sparse matrix of type '<class 'numpy.int64'>'
            with 4354 stored elements in Compressed Sparse Row format>
```

There are 350 rows, which means we have 350 different comments and 1,418 words. 1418 word apparently are word that appear across all of these phrases.

Now let's print a single comment and then run the analyzer on that comment so that we can see how well the phrases breaks it apart. As seen in the following screenshot, the comment has been printed first and then we are analyzing it below, which is just to see how it broke it into words:

```
print(d['CONTENT'][349])
analyze d['CONTENT'][349]
```

```
The first billion viewed this because they thought it was really cool, the  other billion and a half came to see how stupid t
he first billion were...

['the',
 'first',
 'billion',
 'viewed',
 'this',
 'because',
 'they',
 'thought',
 'it',
 'was',
 'really',
 'cool',
 'the',
 'other',
 'billion',
 'and',
 'half',
```

We can use the vectorizer feature to find out which word the dataset found after vectorizing. The following is the result found after vectorizing where it starts with numbers and ends with regular words:

```
In [11]: vectorizer.get_feature_names()

Out[11]: ['00',
          '000',
          '02',
          '034',
          '05',
          '08',
          '10',
          '100',
          '100000415527985',
          '102000253113705769',
          '1030',
          '1073741828',
          '11',
          '1111',
          '112720997191206369631',
          '12',
          '123',
          '124',
          '124923004',
```

Execute the following command to shuffle the dataset with fraction 100% that is adding `frac=1`:

```
In [12]:  dshuf = d.sample(frac=1)
```

Now we will split the dataset into training and testing sets. Let's assume that the first 300 will be for training, while the latter 50 will be for testing:

```
In [13]:  d_train = dshuf[:300]
          d_test = dshuf[300:]
          d_train_att = vectorizer.fit_transform(d_train['CONTENT']) # fit bag-of-words on training set
          d_test_att = vectorizer.transform(d_test['CONTENT']) # reuse on testing set
          d_train_label = d_train['CLASS']
          d_test_label = d_test['CLASS']
```

In the preceding code, `vectorizer.fit_transform(d_train['CONTENT'])` is an important step. At that stage, you have a training set that you want to perform a fit transform on, which means it will learn the words and also produce the matrix. However, for the testing set, we don't perform a fit transform again, since we don't want the model to learn different words for the testing data. We will use the same words that it learned on the training set. Suppose that the testing set has different words out of which some of them are unique to the testing set that might have never appeared in the training set. That's perfectly fine and anyhow we are going to ignore it. Because we are using the training set to build a random forest or decision tree or whatever would be the case, we have to use a certain set of words, and those words will have to be the same words, used on the testing set. We cannot introduce new words to the testing set since the random forest or any other model would not be able to gauge the new words.

Now we perform the transform on the dataset, and later we will use the answers for training and testing. The training set now has 300 rows and 1,287 different words or columns, and the testing set has 50 rows, but we have the same 1,287 columns:

```
In [14]:  d_train_att

Out[14]:  <300x1253 sparse matrix of type '<class 'numpy.int64'>'
                  with 3720 stored elements in Compressed Sparse Row format>


In [15]:  d_test_att

Out[15]:  <50x1253 sparse matrix of type '<class 'numpy.int64'>'
                  with 467 stored elements in Compressed Sparse Row format>
```

Even though the testing set has different words, we need to make sure it is transformed in the same way as the training set with the same columns. Now we will begin with the building of the random forest classifier. We will be converting this dataset into 80 different trees and we will fit the training set so that we can score its performance on the testing set:

```
In [16]:  from sklearn.ensemble import RandomForestClassifier
          clf = RandomForestClassifier(n_estimators=80)


In [17]:  clf.fit(d_train_att, d_train_label)

Out[17]:  RandomForestClassifier(bootstrap=True, class_weight=None, criterion='gini',
                  max_depth=None, max_features='auto', max_leaf_nodes=None,
                  min_impurity_decrease=0.0, min_impurity_split=None,
                  min_samples_leaf=1, min_samples_split=2,
                  min_weight_fraction_leaf=0.0, n_estimators=80, n_jobs=1,
                  oob_score=False, random_state=None, verbose=0,
                  warm_start=False)


In [18]:  clf.score(d_test_att, d_test_label)

Out[18]:  0.97999999999999998
```

The output of the score that we received is 98%; that's really good. Here it seems it got confused between spam and not-spam. We need be sure that the accuracy is high; for that, we will perform a cross validation with five different splits. To perform a cross validation, we will use all the training data and let it split it into four different groups: 20%, 80%, and 20% will be testing data, and 80% will be the training data:

```
In [19]:  from sklearn.metrics import confusion_matrix
          pred_labels = clf.predict(d_test_att)
          confusion_matrix(d_test_label, pred_labels)

Out[19]:  array([[26,  0],
                 [ 1, 23]], dtype=int64)

In [20]:  from sklearn.model_selection import cross_val_score
          scores = cross_val_score(clf, d_train_att, d_train_label, cv=5)
          # show average score and +/- two standard deviations away (covering 95% of scores)
          print("Accuracy: %0.2f (+/- %0.2f)" % (scores.mean(), scores.std() * 2))

          Accuracy: 0.97 (+/- 0.03)
```

We will now perform an average to the scores that we just obtained, which comes to about 95% accuracy. Now we will print all the data as seen in the following screenshot:

```
In [22]:  # load all datasets and combine them
          d = pd.concat([pd.read_csv("D:/Chapter04/Youtube01-Psy.csv"),
                         pd.read_csv("D:/Chapter04/Youtube02-KatyPerry.csv"),
                         pd.read_csv("D:/Chapter04/Youtube03-LMFAO.csv"),
                         pd.read_csv("D:/Chapter04/Youtube04-Eminem.csv"),
                         pd.read_csv("D:/Chapter04/Youtube05-Shakira.csv")])

In [23]:  len(d)

Out[23]:  1956
```

The entire dataset has five different videos with comments, which means all together we have around 2,000 rows. On checking all the comments, we noticed that there are 1005 spam comments and 951 not-spam comments, that quite close enough to split it in to even parts:

```
In [24]: len(d.query('CLASS == 1'))

Out[24]: 1005

In [25]: len(d.query('CLASS == 0'))

Out[25]: 951
```

Here we will shuffle the entire dataset and separate the comments and the answers:

```
In [26]: dshuf = d.sample(frac=1)
         d_content = dshuf['CONTENT']
         d_label = dshuf['CLASS']
```

We need to perform a couple of steps here with CountVectorizer followed by the random forest. For this, we will use a feature in scikit-learn called a **Pipeline**. Pipeline is really convenient and will bring together two or more steps so that all the steps are treated as one. So, we will build a pipeline with the bag of words, and then use countVectorizer followed by the random forest classifier. Then we will print the pipeline, and it the steps required:

```
In [27]: # set up a pipeline
         from sklearn.pipeline import Pipeline, make_pipeline
         pipeline = Pipeline([
             ('bag-of-words', CountVectorizer()),
             ('random forest', RandomForestClassifier()),
         ])
         pipeline

Out[27]: Pipeline(memory=None,
             steps=[('bag-of-words', CountVectorizer(analyzer='word', binary=False, decode_error='strict',
                 dtype=<class 'numpy.int64'>, encoding='utf-8', input='content',
                 lowercase=True, max_df=1.0, max_features=None, min_df=1,
                 ngram_range=(1, 1), preprocessor=None, stop_words=None,
             ...n_jobs=1,
                     oob_score=False, random_state=None, verbose=0,
                     warm_start=False))])
```

We can let the pipeline name of each step by itself by adding `CountVectorizer` in our `RandomForestClassifier` and it will name them `CountVectorizer` and `RandomForestclassifier`:

```
In [28]:   # or: pipeline = make_pipeline(CountVectorizer(), RandomForestClassifier())
           make_pipeline(CountVectorizer(), RandomForestClassifier())

Out[28]:   Pipeline(memory=None,
                steps=[('countvectorizer', CountVectorizer(analyzer='word', binary=False, decode_error='strict',
                    dtype=<class 'numpy.int64'>, encoding='utf-8', input='content',
                    lowercase=True, max_df=1.0, max_features=None, min_df=1,
                    ngram_range=(1, 1), preprocessor=None, stop_words=None,
                ...n_jobs=1,
                    oob_score=False, random_state=None, verbose=0,
                    warm_start=False))])
```

Once the pipeline is created you can just call it fit and it will perform the rest that is first it perform the fit and then transform with the `CountVectorizer`, followed by a fit with the `RandomForest` classifier. That's the benefit of having a pipeline:

```
In [29]:   pipeline.fit(d_content[:1500],d_label[:1500])

Out[29]:   Pipeline(memory=None,
                steps=[('bag-of-words', CountVectorizer(analyzer='word', binary=False, decode_error='strict',
                    dtype=<class 'numpy.int64'>, encoding='utf-8', input='content',
                    lowercase=True, max_df=1.0, max_features=None, min_df=1,
                    ngram_range=(1, 1), preprocessor=None, stop_words=None,
                ...n_jobs=1,
                    oob_score=False, random_state=None, verbose=0,
                    warm_start=False))])
```

Now you call score so that it knows that when we are scoring it will to run it through the bag of words `countVectorizer`, followed by predicting with the `RandomForestClassifier`:

```
In [30]:   pipeline.score(d_content[1500:], d_label[1500:])

Out[30]:   0.93859649122807021
```

This whole procedure will produce a score of about 94. We can only predict a single example with the pipeline. For example, imagine we have a new comment after the dataset has been trained, and we want to know whether the user has just typed this comment or whether it's spam:

```
In [31]: pipeline.predict(["what a neat video!"])

Out[31]: array([0], dtype=int64)
```

As seen, it's detected correctly; but what about the following comment:

```
In [32]: pipeline.predict(["plz subscribe to my channel"])

Out[32]: array([1], dtype=int64)
```

To overcome this and deploy this classifier into an environment and predict whether it is a spm or not when someone types a new comment. We will use our pipeline to figure out how accurate our cross-validation was. We find in this case that the average accuracy was about 94:

```
In [33]: scores = cross_val_score(pipeline, d_content, d_label, cv=5)
         print("Accuracy: %0.2f (+/- %0.2f)" % (scores.mean(), scores.std() * 2))

         Accuracy: 0.94 (+/- 0.02)
```

It's pretty good. Now let's add TF-IDF to our model to make it more precise:

```
In [34]: # add tfidf
         from sklearn.feature_extraction.text import TfidfTransformer
         pipeline2 = make_pipeline(CountVectorizer(),
                                   TfidfTransformer(norm=None),
                                   RandomForestClassifier())
```

This will be placed after countVectorizer. After we have produced the counts, we can then produce a TF-IDF score for these counts. Now we will add this in the pipeline and perform another cross-validation check with the same accuracy:

```
In [35]: scores = cross_val_score(pipeline2, d_content, d_label, cv=5)
         print("Accuracy: %0.2f (+/- %0.2f)" % (scores.mean(), scores.std() * 2))

         Accuracy: 0.94 (+/- 0.03)
```

This show the steps required for the pipeline:

```
In [36]:   pipeline2.steps

Out[36]:   [('countvectorizer',
            CountVectorizer(analyzer='word', binary=False, decode_error='strict',
                dtype=<class 'numpy.int64'>, encoding='utf-8', input='content',
                lowercase=True, max_df=1.0, max_features=None, min_df=1,
                ngram_range=(1, 1), preprocessor=None, stop_words=None,
                strip_accents=None, token_pattern='(?u)\\b\\w\\w+\\b',
                tokenizer=None, vocabulary=None)),
           ('tfidftransformer',
            TfidfTransformer(norm=None, smooth_idf=True, sublinear_tf=False, use_idf=True)),
           ('randomforestclassifier',
            RandomForestClassifier(bootstrap=True, class_weight=None, criterion='gini',
                max_depth=None, max_features='auto', max_leaf_nodes=None,
                min_impurity_decrease=0.0, min_impurity_split=None,
                min_samples_leaf=1, min_samples_split=2,
                min_weight_fraction_leaf=0.0, n_estimators=10, n_jobs=1,
                oob_score=False, random_state=None, verbose=0,
                warm_start=False))]
```

The following output got us `CountVectorizer`, a TF-IDF transformer, and `RandomForestClassifier`. Notice that `countvectorizer` can be lower case or upper case in the dataset; it is on us to decide how many words you want to have. We can either use single words or bigrams, which would be pairs of words, or trigrams, which can be triples of words. We can also remove stop words, which are really common English words such as **and**, **or**, and **the**. With TF-IDF, you can turn off the `idf` component and just keep the `tf` component, which would just be a log of the count. You can use `idf` as well. With random forests, you've got a choice of how many trees you use, which is the number of estimators.

There's another feature of scikit-learn available that allows us to search all of these parameters. For that, it finds out what the best parameters are:

```
In [37]:   # parameter search
           parameters = {
               'countvectorizer__max_features': (None, 1000, 2000),
               'countvectorizer__ngram_range': ((1, 1), (1, 2)),   # unigrams or bigrams
               'countvectorizer__stop_words': ('english', None),
               'tfidftransformer__use_idf': (True, False), # effectively turn on/off tfidf
               'randomforestclassifier__n_estimators': (20, 50, 100)
           }
           from sklearn.model_selection import GridSearchCV
           grid_search = GridSearchCV(pipeline2, parameters, n_jobs=-1, verbose=1)
```

We can make a little dictionary where we say the name of the pipeline step and then mention what the parameter name would be and this gives us our options. For demonstration, we are going to try maximum number of words or maybe just a maximum of 1,000 or 2,000 words.

Using `ngrams`, we can mention just single words or pairs of words that are stop words, use the English dictionary of stop words, or don't use stop words, which means in the first case we need to get rid of common words, and in the second case we do not get rid of common words. Using TF-IDF, we use `idf` to state whether it's yes or no. The random forest we created uses 20, 50, or 100 trees. Using this, we can perform a grid search, which runs through all of the combinations of parameters and finds out what the best combination is. So, let's give our pipeline number 2, which has the TF-IDF along with it. We will use `fit` to perform the search and the outcome can be seen in the following screenshot:

```
In [38]: grid_search.fit(d_content, d_label)

         Fitting 3 folds for each of 72 candidates, totalling 216 fits

         [Parallel(n_jobs=-1)]: Done  42 tasks      | elapsed:   6.6s
         [Parallel(n_jobs=-1)]: Done 192 tasks      | elapsed:  22.0s
         [Parallel(n_jobs=-1)]: Done 216 out of 216 | elapsed:  25.0s finished

Out[38]: GridSearchCV(cv=None, error_score='raise',
                estimator=Pipeline(memory=None,
             steps=[('countvectorizer', CountVectorizer(analyzer='word', binary=False, decode_error='strict',
                 dtype=<class 'numpy.int64'>, encoding='utf-8', input='content',
                 lowercase=True, max_df=1.0, max_features=None, min_df=1,
                 ngram_range=(1, 1), preprocessor=None, stop_words=None,
           ...n_jobs=1,
                     oob_score=False, random_state=None, verbose=0,
                     warm_start=False))]),
                fit_params=None, iid=True, n_jobs=-1,
                param_grid={'countvectorizer__max_features': (None, 1000, 2000), 'countvectorizer__ngram_range': ((1, 1), (1, 2)), 'count
         vectorizer__stop_words': ('english', None), 'tfidftransformer__use_idf': (True, False), 'randomforestclassifier__n_estimators':
         (20, 50, 100)},
                pre_dispatch='2*n_jobs', refit=True, return_train_score='warn',
                scoring=None, verbose=1)
```

Since there is a large number of words, it takes a little while, around 40 seconds, and ultimately finds the best parameters. We can get the best parameters out of the grid search and print them to see what the score is:

```
In [39]: print("Best score: %0.3f" % grid_search.best_score_)
         print("Best parameters set:")
         best_parameters = grid_search.best_estimator_.get_params()
         for param_name in sorted(parameters.keys()):
             print("\t%s: %r" % (param_name, best_parameters[param_name]))

Best score: 0.963
Best parameters set:
        countvectorizer__max_features: 1000
        countvectorizer__ngram_range: (1, 1)
        countvectorizer__stop_words: 'english'
        randomforestclassifier__n_estimators: 50
        tfidftransformer__use_idf: True
```

So, we got nearly 96% accuracy. We used around 1,000 words, only single words, used yes to get rid of stop words, had 100 trees in the random forest, and used yes and the IDF and the TF-IDF computation. Here we've demonstrated not only bag of words, TF-IDF, and random forest, but also the pipeline feature and the parameter search feature known as grid search.

Word2Vec models

In this section, we'll learn about Word2Vec, a modern and popular technique for working with text. Usually, Word2Vec performs better than simple bag of words models. A bag of words model only counts how many times each word appears in each document. Given two such bag of words vectors, we can compare documents to see how similar they are. This is the same as comparing the words used in the documents. In other words, if the two documents have many similar words that appear a similar number of times, they will be considered similar.

But bag of words models have no information about how similar the words are. So, if two documents do not use exactly the same words but do use synonyms, such as **please** and **plz**, they're not regarded as similar for the bag of words model. Word2Vec can figure out that some words are similar to each other and we can exploit that fact to get better performance when doing machine learning with text.

In Word2Vec, each word itself is a vector, with perhaps 300 dimensions. For example, in a pre-trained Google Word2Vec model that examined millions or billions of pages of text, we can see that cat, dog, and spatula are 300-dimensional vectors:

- Cat = <0.012, 0.204, ..., -0.275, 0.056> (300 dimensions)
- Dog = <0.051, -0.022, ..., -0.355, 0.227>
- Spatula = <-0.191, -0.043, ..., -0.348, 0.398>
- Similarity (distance) between cat and dog—0.761
- Similarity between cat and spatula—0.124

If we compare the similarity of the dog and cat vectors, we will get 0.761 or 76% of similarity. If we do the same with cat and spatula, we get 0.124. It's clear that Word2Vec learned that dog and cat are similar words but cat and spatula are not. Word2Vec uses neural networks to learn these word vectors. At a high level, a neural network is similar to random forest or a decision tree and other machine learning techniques because they're given a bunch of inputs and a bunch of outputs, and they learn how to predict the outputs from the inputs.

For Word2Vec, the input is a single word, the word whose vector we want to learn, and the output is its nearby words from the text. Word2Vec also supports the reverse of this input-output configuration. Thus, Word2Vec learns the word vectors by remembering its context words. So, dog and cat will have similar word vectors because these two words are used in similar ways, like *she pet the dog* and *she pet the cat*. Neural networking with Word2Vec can take one of two forms because Word2Vec supports two different techniques for training.

The first technique is known as continuous bag of words, where the context words are the input, leaving out the middle word and the word whose vector we're learning, the middle word, is the output. In the following diagram, you can see three words before and after the word **channel**:

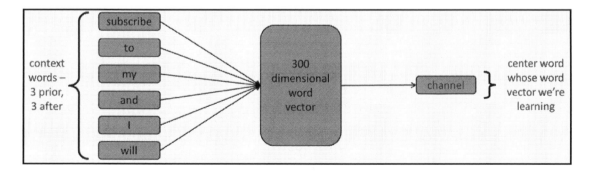

Those are the context words. The continuous bag of words model slides over the whole sentence with every word acting as a center word in turn. The neural network learns the 300-dimensional vectors for each word so that the vector can predict the center word given the context words. In other words, it can predict the output given its inputs.

In the second technique, we're going to flip this. This is known as **skip-gram**, and the center word is the input and the context words are the outputs:

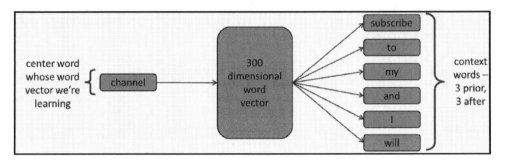

In this technique, the center word vector is used to predict the context words given that center word.

Both of these techniques perform well for most situations. They each have minor pros and cons that will not be important for our use case.

Doc2Vec

We're going to use Word2Vec to detect positive and negative product, restaurant, and movie reviews. We will do so with a slightly different form of Word2Vec known as **Doc2Vec**. In this case, the input is a document name, such as the filename, and the output is the sliding window of the words from the document. This time, we will not have a center word:

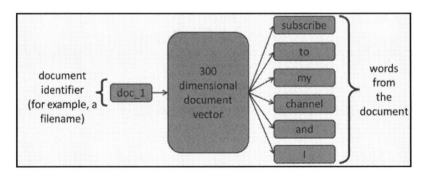

In this case, as a vector that helps us predict the words, from knowing the filename. In fact, the input is not very important, which in this case is the filename. We just need to keep track of the words on the right side, and that they all came from the same document. So, all of those words will be connected to that filename, but the actual content of that filename is not important. Since we can predict the document's words based on its filename, we can effectively have a model that knows which words go together in a document. In other words, that documents usually talk about just one thing, for example, learning that a lot of different positive words are used in positive reviews and a lot of negative words are used in negative reviews.

Document vector

After training, we have a new document and we want to find its document vector. We'll use the word similarities learned during training to construct a vector that will predict the words in the new document. We will use a dummy filename since the actual name is not important. What's important is that it's just one name. So, all of these words get connected together under that one name:

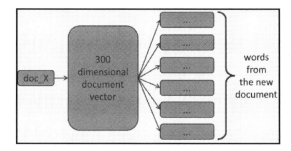

Once we get that new document vector, we can compare it with other document vectors and find which known document from the past is the most similar, as follows:

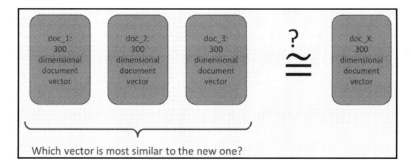

Thus, we can use Doc2Vec to find which documents are most similar to each other. This will help us detect positive and negative reviews because, ideally, the positive reviews will have document vectors that are similar to each other and this will be the same for negative reviews. We expect Doc2Vec to perform better than bag of words because Doc2Vec learns the words that are used together in the same document, so those words that are similar to bag of words never actually learned any information about how similar the words are different.

Detecting positive or negative sentiments in user reviews

In this section, we're going to look at detecting positive and negative sentiments in user reviews. In other words, we are going to detect whether the user is typing a positive comment or a negative comment about the product or service. We're going to use Word2Vec and Doc2Vec specifically and the gensim Python library for those services. There are two categories, which are positive and negative, and we have over 3,000 different reviews to look at. These come from Yelp, IMDb, and Amazon. Let's begin the code by importing the gensim library, which provides Word2Vec and Doc2Vec for logging to note status of the messages:

```
In [1]: import gensim, logging

In [2]: logging.basicConfig(format='%(asctime)s : %(levelname)s : %(message)s', level=logging.INFO)

In [3]: gmodel = gensim.models.KeyedVectors.load_word2vec_format('GoogleNews-vectors-negative300.bin', binary=True)
        2017-11-12 16:06:33,788 : INFO : loading projection weights from GoogleNews-vectors-negative300.bin
        2017-11-12 16:08:10,091 : INFO : loaded (3000000, 300) matrix from GoogleNews-vectors-negative300.bin
```

First, we will see how to load a pre-built Word2Vec model, provided by Google, that has been trained on billions of pages of text and has ultimately produced 300-dimensional vectors for all the different words. Once the model is loaded, we will look at the vector for cat. This shows that the model is a 300-dimensional vector, as represented by the word cat:

```
In [4]: gmodel['cat']

Out[4]: array([ 0.0123291 ,  0.20410156, -0.28515625,  0.21679688,  0.11816406,
        0.08300781,  0.04980469, -0.00952148,  0.22070312, -0.12597656,
        0.08056641, -0.5859375 , -0.00445557, -0.296875  , -0.01312256,
       -0.08349609,  0.05053711,  0.15136719, -0.44921875, -0.0135498 ,
        0.21484375, -0.14746094,  0.22460938, -0.125     , -0.09716797,
        0.24902344, -0.2890625 ,  0.36523438,  0.41210938, -0.0859375 ,
       -0.07861328, -0.19726562, -0.09082031, -0.14160156, -0.10253906,
        0.13085938, -0.00346375,  0.07226562,  0.04418945,  0.34570312,
        0.07470703, -0.11230469,  0.06738281,  0.11230469,  0.01977539,
       -0.12353516,  0.20996094, -0.07226562, -0.02783203,  0.05541992,
       -0.33398438,  0.08544922,  0.34375   ,  0.13964844,  0.04931641,
       -0.13476562,  0.16308594, -0.37304688,  0.39648438,  0.10693359,
        0.22167969,  0.21289062, -0.08984375,  0.20703125,  0.08935547,
       -0.08251953,  0.05957031,  0.10205078, -0.19238281, -0.09082031,
        0.4921875 ,  0.03955078, -0.07080078, -0.0019989 , -0.23046875,
        0.25585938,  0.08984375, -0.10644531,  0.00105286, -0.05883789,
        0.05102539, -0.0291748 ,  0.19335938, -0.14160156, -0.33398438,
        0.08154297, -0.27539062,  0.10058594, -0.10449219, -0.12353516,
       -0.140625  ,  0.03491211, -0.11767578, -0.1796875 , -0.21484375,
       -0.23828125,  0.08447266, -0.07519531, -0.25976562, -0.21289062,
       -0.22363281, -0.09716797,  0.11572266,  0.15429688,  0.07373047,
       -0.27539062,  0.14257812, -0.0201416 ,  0.10009766, -0.19042969,
       -0.09375   ,  0.14160156,  0.17089844,  0.3125    , -0.16699219,
```

The following screenshot shows the 300-dimensional vector for the word dog:

```
In [5]: gmodel['dog']

Out[5]: array([  5.12695312e-02,  -2.23388672e-02,  -1.72851562e-01,
         1.61132812e-01,  -8.44726562e-02,   5.73730469e-02,
         5.85937500e-02,  -8.25195312e-02,  -1.53808594e-02,
        -6.34765625e-02,   1.79687500e-01,  -4.23828125e-01,
        -2.25830078e-02,  -1.66015625e-01,  -2.51464844e-02,
         1.07421875e-01,  -1.99218750e-01,   1.59179688e-01,
        -1.87500000e-01,  -1.20117188e-01,   1.55273438e-01,
        -9.91210938e-02,   1.42578125e-01,  -1.64062500e-01,
        -8.93554688e-02,   2.00195312e-01,  -1.49414062e-01,
         3.20312500e-01,   3.28125000e-01,   2.44140625e-02,
        -9.71679688e-02,  -8.20312500e-02,  -3.63769531e-02,
        -8.59375000e-02,  -9.86328125e-02,   7.78198242e-03,
        -1.34277344e-02,   5.27343750e-02,   1.48437500e-01,
         3.33984375e-01,   1.66015625e-02,  -2.12890625e-01,
        -1.50756836e-02,   5.24902344e-02,  -1.07421875e-01,
        -8.88671875e-02,   2.49023438e-01,  -7.03125000e-02,
        -1.59912109e-02,   7.56835938e-02,  -7.03125000e-02,
         1.19140625e-01,   2.29492188e-01,   1.41601562e-02,
         1.15234375e-01,   7.50732422e-03,   2.75390625e-01,
        -2.44140625e-01,   2.96875000e-01,   3.49121094e-02,
         2.42187500e-01,   1.35742188e-01,   1.42578125e-01,
```

The following screenshot shows the 300-dimensional vector for the word `spatula`:

```
In [6]:  gmodel['spatula']

Out[6]:  array([-0.19140625, -0.04296875,  0.27539062,  0.00488281, -0.3203125 ,
                 0.08203125,  0.05566406, -0.03613281, -0.31445312,  0.10693359,
                -0.359375  ,  0.29882812,  0.02331543,  0.05517578, -0.140625  ,
                 0.1953125 , -0.23632812, -0.22167969, -0.06542969, -0.3359375 ,
                 0.25195312, -0.09326172,  0.54296875,  0.11328125, -0.28710938,
                -0.12011719, -0.11181641,  0.20996094, -0.33203125,  0.30273438,
                -0.3359375 , -0.12255859,  0.12890625, -0.28515625, -0.04223633,
                 0.25585938,  0.3203125 ,  0.07177734,  0.19042969, -0.01379395,
                 0.16992188, -0.22460938,  0.5078125 ,  0.08398438, -0.07519531,
                -0.06396484,  0.05371094,  0.34570312,  0.46289062, -0.16699219,
                -0.30664062,  0.15234375, -0.09765625, -0.26171875, -0.14160156,
                 0.2265625 ,  0.49609375, -0.10791016, -0.08447266,  0.234375  ,
                 0.04931641, -0.07128906,  0.05273438, -0.11914062,  0.09814453,
                 0.11181641, -0.13574219, -0.46875   ,  0.26171875,  0.12158203,
                 0.31445312,  0.05810547,  0.0703125 , -0.10107422, -0.27734375,
                -0.16796875, -0.07128906, -0.08007812,  0.07226562, -0.1484375 ,
```

We obtain a result of 76% when computing the similarity of dog and cat, as follows:

```
In [7]:  gmodel.similarity('cat', 'dog')

Out[7]:  0.76094570897822089
```

The similarity between cat and spatula is 12%; it is a bit lower, as it should be:

```
In [8]:  gmodel.similarity('cat', 'spatula')

Out[8]:  0.12412612600429632
```

Here we train our `Word2Vec` and `Doc2Vec` model using the following code:

```
In [9]:  from gensim.models.doc2vec import TaggedDocument
         from gensim.models import Doc2Vec
```

We are using `Doc2Vec` because we want to determine a vector for each document, not necessarily for each word in the document, because our documents are reviews and we want to see whether these reviews are positive or negative, which means it's similar to positive reviews or similar to negative reviews. `Doc2Vec` is provided by `gensim` and the library has a class called `TaggedDocument` that allows us to use "these are the words in the document, and Doc2Vec is the model".

Now we create a utility function that will take a sentence or a whole paragraph and lowercase it and remove all the HTML tags, apostrophes, punctuation, spaces, and repeated spaces, and then ultimately break it apart by words:

```
In [10]:  def extract_words(sent):
              sent = sent.lower()
              sent = re.sub(r'<[^>]+>', ' ', sent) # strip html tags
              sent = re.sub(r'(\w)\'(\w)', '\1\2', sent) # remove apostrophes
              sent = re.sub(r'\W', ' ', sent) # remove punctuation
              sent = re.sub(r'\s+', ' ', sent) # remove repeated spaces
              sent = sent.strip()
              return sent.split()
```

Now it's time for our training set. We are not going to use the 3,000 Yelp, IMDb, and Amazon reviews because there's simply not enough data to train for a good `Doc2Vec` model. If we had millions reviews, then we could take a good portion of that to train with and use the rest for testing, but with just 3,000 reviews it's not enough. So, instead, I've gathered reviews from IMDb and other places, including Rotten Tomato. This will be enough to train a `Doc2Vec` model, but none of these are actually from the dataset that we're going to use for our final prediction. These are simply reviews. They're positive; they're negative. I don't know which, as I'm not keeping track of which. What matters is that we have enough text to learn how words are used in these reviews. Nothing records whether the review is positive or negative.

So, `Doc2Vec` and `Word2Vec` are actually being used for unsupervised training. That means we don't have any answers. We simply learn how words are used together. Remember the context of words, and how a word is used according to the words nearby:

```
In [11]:  # unsupervised training data
          import re
          import os
          unsup_sentences = []

          # source: http://ai.stanford.edu/~amaas/data/sentiment/, data from IMDB
          for dirname in ["train/pos", "train/neg", "train/unsup", "test/pos", "test/neg"]:
              for fname in sorted(os.listdir("aclImdb/" + dirname)):
                  if fname[-4:] == '.txt':
                      with open("aclImdb/" + dirname + "/" + fname, encoding='UTF-8') as f:
                          sent = f.read()
                          words = extract_words(sent)
                          unsup_sentences.append(TaggedDocument(words, [dirname + "/" + fname]))

          # source: http://www.cs.cornell.edu/people/pabo/movie-review-data/
          for dirname in ["review_polarity/txt_sentoken/pos", "review_polarity/txt_sentoken/neg"]:
              for fname in sorted(os.listdir(dirname)):
                  if fname[-4:] == '.txt':
                      with open(dirname + "/" + fname, encoding='UTF-8') as f:
                          for i, sent in enumerate(f):
                              words = extract_words(sent)
                              unsup_sentences.append(TaggedDocument(words, ["%s/%s-%d" % (dirname, fname, i)]))

          # source: https://nlp.stanford.edu/sentiment/, data from Rotten Tomatoes
          with open("stanfordSentimentTreebank/original_rt_snippets.txt", encoding='UTF-8') as f:
              for i, line in enumerate(f):
                  words = extract_words(sent)
                  unsup_sentences.append(TaggedDocument(words, ["rt-%d" % i]))
```

So, in each case, in each file, we simply make a `TaggedDocument` object with the words from that document or that review plus a tag, which is simply the filename. This is important so that it learns that all these words go together in the same document, and that these words are somehow related to each other. After loading, we have 175,000 training examples from different documents:

```
In [12]:  len(unsup_sentences)
Out[12]:  175325
```

Now let's have a look at the first 10 sentences in the following screenshot:

```
In [13]: unsup_sentences[0:10]
```

```
Out[13]: [TaggedDocument(words=['bromwell', 'high', 'is', 'a', 'cartoon', 'comedy', 'it', 'ran', 'at', 'the', 'same', 'time', 'as', 's
         ome', 'other', 'programs', 'about', 'school', 'life', 'such', 'as', 'teachers', 'my', '35', 'years', 'in', 'the', 'teaching',
         'profession', 'lead', 'me', 'to', 'believe', 'that', 'bromwell', 'hig', 'satire', 'is', 'much', 'closer', 'to', 'reality', 't
         han', 'is', 'teachers', 'the', 'scramble', 'to', 'survive', 'financially', 'the', 'insightful', 'students', 'who', 'can', 'se
         e', 'right', 'through', 'their', 'pathetic', 'teachers', 'pomp', 'the', 'pettiness', 'of', 'the', 'whole', 'situation', 'al
         l', 'remind', 'me', 'of', 'the', 'schools', 'i', 'knew', 'and', 'their', 'students', 'when', 'i', 'saw', 'the', 'episode', 'i
         n', 'which', 'a', 'student', 'repeatedly', 'tried', 'to', 'burn', 'down', 'the', 'school', 'i', 'immediately', 'recalled', 'a
         t', 'high', 'a', 'classic', 'line', 'inspector', 'here', 'to', 'sack', 'one', 'of', 'your', 'teachers', 'student', 'welcome',
         'to', 'bromwell', 'high', 'i', 'expect', 'that', 'many', 'adults', 'of', 'my', 'age', 'think', 'that', 'bromwell', 'high', 'i
         s', 'far', 'fetched', 'what', 'a', 'pity', 'that', 'it', 'is'], tags=['train/pos/0_9.txt']),
         TaggedDocument(words=['homelessness', 'or', 'houselessness', 'as', 'george', 'carlin', 'stated', 'has', 'been', 'an', 'issu
         e', 'for', 'years', 'but', 'never', 'a', 'plan', 'to', 'help', 'those', 'on', 'the', 'street', 'that', 'were', 'once', 'consi
         dered', 'human', 'who', 'did', 'everything', 'from', 'going', 'to', 'school', 'work', 'or', 'vote', 'for', 'the', 'matter',
         'most', 'people', 'think', 'of', 'the', 'homeless', 'as', 'just', 'a', 'lost', 'cause', 'while', 'worrying', 'about', 'thing
         s', 'such', 'as', 'racism', 'the', 'war', 'on', 'iraq', 'pressuring', 'kids', 'to', 'succeed', 'technology', 'the', 'election
         s', 'inflation', 'or', 'worrying', 'if', 'the', 'l', 'be', 'next', 'to', 'end', 'up', 'on', 'the', 'streets', 'but', 'what',
         'if', 'you', 'were', 'given', 'a', 'bet', 'to', 'live', 'on', 'the', 'streets', 'for', 'a', 'month', 'without', 'the', 'luxur
         ies', 'you', 'once', 'had', 'from', 'a', 'home', 'the', 'entertainment', 'sets', 'a', 'bathroom', 'pictures', 'on', 'the', 'w
         all', 'a', 'computer', 'and', 'everything', 'you', 'once', 'treasure', 'to', 'see', 'what', 'i', 'like', 'to', 'be', 'homeles
```

We shuffle these documents and then feed them into our `Doc2Vec` trainer, using `Doc2Vec(permuter, dm=0, hs=1, size=50)`, where we finally do the training of the `Doc2Vec` model and where it learns the document vectors for all the different documents. `dm=0` and `hs=1` are just parameters to say how to do the training. These are just things that I found were the most accurate. `dm=0` is where we are using the model that was shown in the last section, which means it receives a filename and it predicts the words:

```
In [15]: permuter = PermuteSentences(unsup_sentences)
         model = Doc2Vec(permuter, dm=0, hs=1, size=50)

         2017-11-12 16:09:07,700 : WARNING : consider setting layer size to a multiple of 4 for greater performance
         2017-11-12 16:09:07,703 : INFO : collecting all words and their counts
         2017-11-12 16:09:08,097 : INFO : PROGRESS: at example #0, processed 0 words (0/s), 0 word types, 0 tags
         2017-11-12 16:09:08,837 : INFO : PROGRESS: at example #10000, processed 1389399 words (1882036/s), 44788 word types, 10000 ta
         gs
         2017-11-12 16:09:09,546 : INFO : PROGRESS: at example #20000, processed 2818609 words (2024079/s), 61270 word types, 20000 ta
         gs
         2017-11-12 16:09:10,234 : INFO : PROGRESS: at example #30000, processed 4225040 words (2051374/s), 72774 word types, 30000 ta
         gs
         2017-11-12 16:09:10,921 : INFO : PROGRESS: at example #40000, processed 5632885 words (2057947/s), 82225 word types, 40000 ta
         gs
         2017-11-12 16:09:11,602 : INFO : PROGRESS: at example #50000, processed 7040997 words (2074544/s), 90454 word types, 50000 ta
         gs
         2017-11-12 16:09:12,284 : INFO : PROGRESS: at example #60000, processed 8474509 words (2106160/s), 97853 word types, 60000 ta
         gs
         2017-11-12 16:09:12,983 : INFO : PROGRESS: at example #70000, processed 9855488 words (1983678/s), 104567 word types, 70000 t
         ags
         2017-11-12 16:09:13,669 : INFO : PROGRESS: at example #80000, processed 11260351 words (2053644/s), 110705 word types, 80000
         tags
```

Here `size=50` means that we found that 50-dimensional vectors for each document was best, and 300-dimensional vectors are optimal, because we don't have enough training examples. Since we don't have millions or billions of data. This is a good 300 dimensional vector, and 50 seemed to work better. Running this code uses the processor and all the cores you have, so it will takes some time to execute. You will see that it's going through all the percentages of how much it got through. Ultimately, it takes 300 seconds to get this information in my case, which is definitely not bad. That's pretty fast, but if you have millions or billions of training documents, it could take days.

Once the training is complete, we can delete some stuff to free up some memory:

```
In [16]:  # done with training, free up some memory
          model.delete_temporary_training_data(keep_inference=True)
```

We do need to keep the inference data, which is enough to bind a new document vector for new documents, but we don't need it to keep all the data about all the different words.

You can save the model and then load it later with the `model =`
`Doc2Vec.Load('reviews.d2v')` command, if you want to put it in a product and deploy it, or put it on a server:

```
In [17]:  model.save('reviews.d2v')
          # in other program, we could write: model = Doc2Vec.load('reviews.d2v')

          2017-11-12 16:14:35,953 : INFO : saving Doc2Vec object under reviews.d2v, separately None
          2017-11-12 16:14:35,956 : INFO : not storing attribute syn0norm
          2017-11-12 16:14:35,958 : INFO : not storing attribute cum_table
          2017-11-12 16:14:40,700 : INFO : saved reviews.d2v
```

After the model's been trained, you can infer a vector, which is regarding what the document vector is for this new document. So, let's extract the words with the utility function. Here we are using an example phrase that was found in a review. This is the 50-dimensional vector it learned for that phrase:

```
In [18]:  model.infer_vector(extract_words("This place is not worth your time, let alone Vegas."))

Out[18]:  array([ 0.16600764,  0.29806057, -0.37614173,  0.58661956,  0.31548923,
                 -0.15109532, -0.19294184, -0.80975324, -0.13256417, -0.26431978,
                  0.15649557, -0.36540538, -0.33639464, -0.55479848, -0.02375498,
                  0.12179437, -0.06088163, -0.17349492, -0.19584687,  0.09399831,
                  0.01947556, -0.17546433, -0.07536539, -0.05634249,  0.2418247 ,
                 -0.11649339, -0.18398936, -0.37568066, -0.04755535, -0.23786636,
                  0.35202903, -0.25357839,  0.05126057, -0.22089498,  0.09130105,
                 -0.46730992,  0.34186646,  0.17174301,  0.51055247,  0.21438542,
                 -0.41699263, -0.5968706 , -0.00541743,  0.39446551,  0.07960459,
                 -0.20494871,  0.11499975,  0.22761559,  0.24039924, -0.06279976], dtype=float32)
```

Now the question that rises is what about a negative phrase? And another negative phrases. Are they considered similar? Well, they're considered 48% similar, as seen in the following screenshot:

```
In [19]:  from sklearn.metrics.pairwise import cosine_similarity
          cosine_similarity(
              [model.infer_vector(extract_words("This place is not worth your time, let alone Vegas."))],
              [model.infer_vector(extract_words("Service sucks."))])

Out[19]:  array([[ 0.48211202]], dtype=float32)
```

What about different phrases? `Highly recommended` and `Service sucks`. They're less similar:

```
In [20]:  cosine_similarity(
              [model.infer_vector(extract_words("Highly recommended."))],
              [model.infer_vector(extract_words("Service sucks."))])

Out[20]:  array([[ 0.28899333]], dtype=float32)
```

The model learned about how words are used together in the same review and that these words go together in one way and that other words go together in a different way.

Finally, we are ready to load our real dataset for prediction:

```
In [21]:  sentences = []
          sentvecs = []
          sentiments = []
          for fname in ["yelp", "amazon_cells", "imdb"]:
              with open("sentiment labelled sentences/%s_labelled.txt" % fname, encoding='UTF-8') as f:
                  for i, line in enumerate(f):
                      line_split = line.strip().split('\t')
                      sentences.append(line_split[0])
                      words = extract_words(line_split[0])
                      sentvecs.append(model.infer_vector(words, steps=10)) # create a vector for this document
                      sentiments.append(int(line_split[1]))

          # shuffle sentences, sentvecs, sentiments together
          combined = list(zip(sentences, sentvecs, sentiments))
          random.shuffle(combined)
          sentences, sentvecs, sentiments = zip(*combined)
```

To summarize, we used Yelp, Amazon, and IMDb reviews. We loaded different files and in each file, each line had a review. As a result, we get the words from the line and found out what the vector was for that document. We put that in a list, shuffle, and finally built a classifier. In this case, we're going to use k-nearest neighbors, which is a really simple technique.

It's just a technique that says *find all the similar documents*, in this case, the nine closest documents to the one that we're looking at, and count votes:

```
In [22]:  from sklearn.neighbors import KNeighborsClassifier
          from sklearn.ensemble import RandomForestClassifier
          from sklearn.model_selection import cross_val_score
          import numpy as np

          clf = KNeighborsClassifier(n_neighbors=9)
          clfrf = RandomForestClassifier()
```

We will be using nine reviews for the purposes of this example, and if you have a majority, let's say of positive reviews, then we will say that this is a positive review too. If the majority says negative, then this is a negative too. We don't want a tie regarding the reviews, which is why we say that there's nine instead of eight.

Now we will compare the outcome with a random forest:

```
In [23]:  scores = cross_val_score(clf, sentvecs, sentiments, cv=5)
          np.mean(scores), np.std(scores)

Out[23]:  (0.75900000000000012, 0.016950909513454807)
```

Now we need to perform cross-validation with the 9 nearest neighbors; we get 76% accuracy for detecting positive/negative reviews with Doc2Vec. For experimental purposes, if we use a random forest without really trying to choose an amount of trees, we just get an accuracy of 70%:

```
In [24]:  scores = cross_val_score(clfrf, sentvecs, sentiments, cv=5)
          np.mean(scores), np.std(scores)

Out[24]:  (0.69766666666666655, 0.019988885800753264)
```

In such cases, k-nearest neighbors is both simpler and more accurate. Ultimately, is it all worth it? Well, let's comparing it to the bag of words model. Let's make a little pipeline with CountVectorizer, TF-IDF, and random forest, and at the end, do cross-validation on the same data, which in this case is the reviews. Here, we get 74%, as seen in the following screenshot:

```
In [25]:   # bag-of-words comparison
           from sklearn.pipeline import make_pipeline
           from sklearn.feature_extraction.text import CountVectorizer, TfidfTransformer
           pipeline = make_pipeline(CountVectorizer(), TfidfTransformer(), RandomForestClassifier())

In [26]:   scores = cross_val_score(pipeline, sentences, sentiments, cv=5)
           np.mean(scores), np.std(scores)

Out[26]:   (0.73733333333333329, 0.015937377450509209)
```

The outcome that we found after executing the model build we found Doc2Vec was better. Doc2Vec can be a lot more accurate than bag of words if we add a lot of training examples that are of the same style as the testing set. Hence, in our case, the testing set was pretty much the Yelp, Amazon, and IMDb reviews, which are all one sentence or one line of text and are pretty short. However, the training set that we found came from different reviews from different places, and we got about 175,000 examples. Those were often like paragraphs or just written in different ways.

Ideally, we will train a Doc2Vec or Word2Vec model on examples that are similar to what we're going to predict on later, but it can be difficult to find enough examples, as it was here so we did our best. Even so, it still turned out better than bag of words.

Summary

In this chapter, we introduced text processing and the bag of words technique. We then used this technique to build a spam detector for YouTube comments. Next, we learned about the sophisticated Word2Vec model and put it to task with a coding project that detects positive and negative product, restaurant, and movie reviews. That's the end of this chapter about text.

In the next chapter, we're going to look at deep learning, which is a popular technique that's used in neural networks.

4
Neural Networks

In this chapter, we will get an overview on neural networks. We will see what a simple shallow neural network is and get some familiarity with how they work. We will do this by trying to identify the genre of a song using a shallow neural network. We will also recall our previous work on the spam detector to use the neural network. Further on, we will take a look at larger neural networks, known as **deep learning**, and apply what is known as a convolutional neural network to identify handwritten mathematical symbols. Finally we will revisit the bird species identifier covered previously and use deep learning to produce a much more accurate identifier.

The topics that we will be covering in this chapter are as follows:

- Understanding neural networks
- Identifying the genre of a song using neural networks
- Recalling our work on the spam detector to use neural networks

Understanding neural networks

Neural networks, which were originally called artificial neural networks, are inspired by actual neurons found in animal's brains and other parts of the nervous system. Neurons are connected to each other and they receive and send impulses throughout the animal's body, or in the case of computing, the network.

The following diagram shows the components of a single neuron:

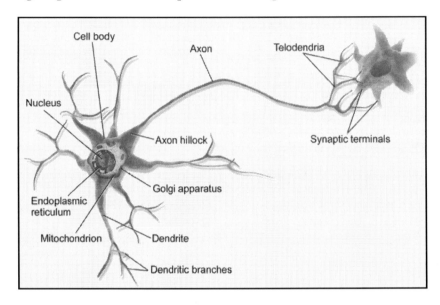

Components of a single neuron

The following graph shows how a neuron fires:

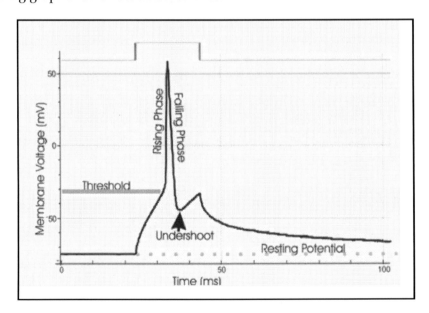

How a neuron fires

It is all or nothing, meaning, when the neuron gets enough input from its neighbors, it quickly fires and sends a signal down its axon to each forward-connected neuron.

Here, we can see actual neurons in a brain:

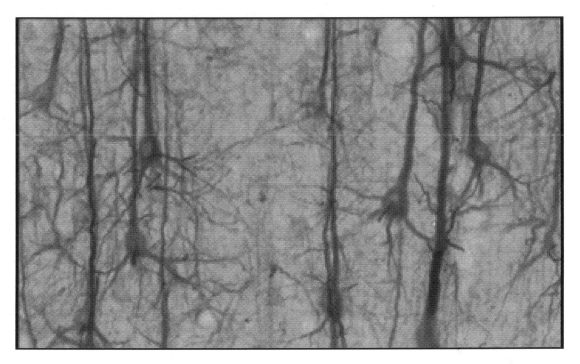

Actual neurons in a brain

A human brain has about 100 billion neurons all together, and has about 100 trillion connections. It is worth noting that the neural networks we create in software have at least 1 million times less complexity.

Feed-forward neural networks

Most of the neural networks that we design are feed forward and fully connected. This means that every neuron connects to every neuron in the next layer. The first layer receives inputs and the last layer gives outputs. The structure of the network, meaning the neuron counts and their connections, is decided ahead of time and cannot change, at least not during training. Also, every input must have the same number of values. This means that images, for example, may need to be resized to match the number of input neurons. The number of neurons in each layer is that layer's shape:

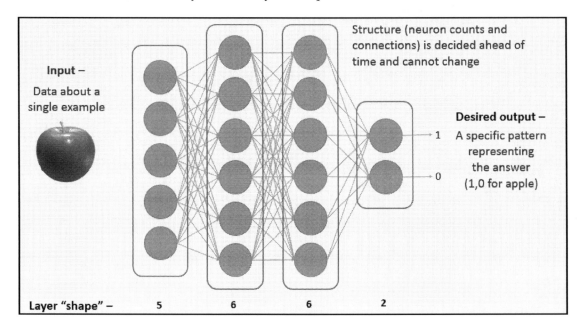

Feed-forward neural design

Each individual neuron adds up the values it receives from the prior layer. Each connection from one neuron to the next has a weight. When adding the inputs, the inputs are multiplied by the respective weights. Each neuron also has an extra input called a **bias**, which is not connected to any other neurons. Once the weighted inputs have been added, an activation function is applied to the sum.

There are several common activation functions, for example, the hyperbolic tangent, whose shape is shown here:

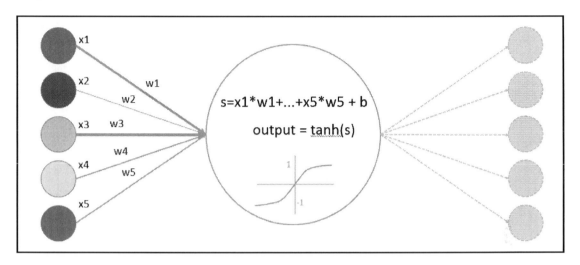

Hyperbolic tangent

The output of each neuron is whatever comes out of the activation function.

The connection waits in a network start random and are adjusted during training. The purpose of training is to examine hundreds, or thousands, or even more example cases and adjust the network's weights until the network is sufficiently accurate.

After training, we have a network structure that we have already defined, and all the weights that were learned during training. As such, the following is true:

A trained neural network = Structure + Learned weights

This is shown here:

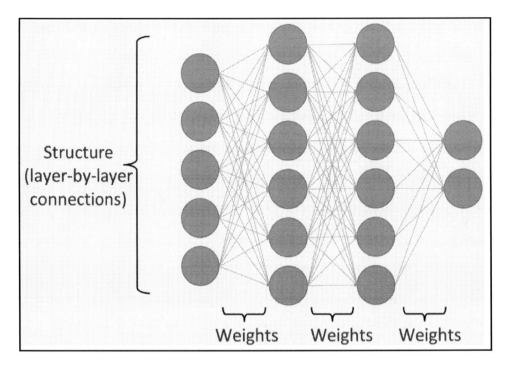

Network structure after training with weights

Now the network is ready to use on new data outside the training set.

Training proceeds in batches, which means that several training cases are sent through the network and the outputs, called **predictions**, are collected. Then, the loss is computed for each batch, which is the measure of the overall error:

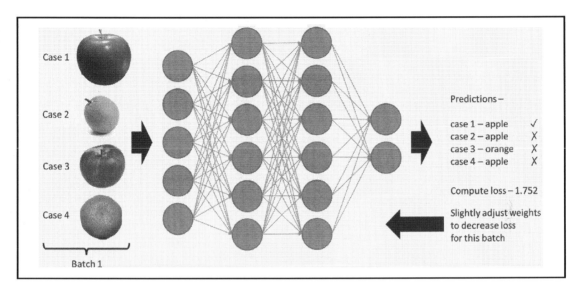

Training procedure: evaluate a batch, adjust weights, and repeat

Each weight in the network is then adjusted depending on whether and how much that weight contributed to the overall loss. With very gradual adjustments, it should be the case that when examples in this batch are visited again, predictions will be more accurate.

The network is often trained over several epochs. By an epoch, we mean all the training data having been processed once. So, 10 epochs means looking at the same training data 10 times. We often segregate 20% or so of the training data as a validation set. This is data that we don't use during training and instead only use to evaluate the model after each epoch.

Ideally, we want the network to become more accurate, which means we want to decrease loss, and this should be true for both the training set and the validation set.

The following set of graph shows this ideal kind of behavior:

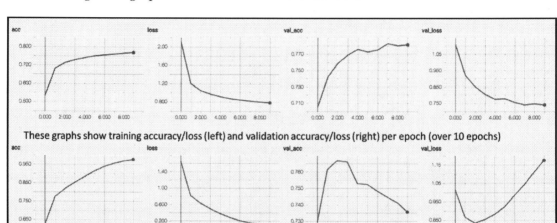

Ideal behavior

Note the signs of overfitting, meaning training loss goes down but validation loss goes up.

If the network is not designed correctly, for example, if it has too many layers, the network may overfit, meaning it performs very well in the training set but poorly on the validation set. This is an issue because ultimately we want to use the neural network on new data from the real world, which will probably be a little different than the training set, hence we use a validation set to see how well the network performs on data it didn't see for training.

Identifying the genre of a song with neural networks

In this section, we're going to build a neural network that can identify the genre of a song. We will use the GTZAN Genre Collection (`http://marsyasweb.appspot.com/download/data_sets/.GTZAN Genre Collection`). It has 1,000 different songs from over 10 different genres. There are 100 songs per genre and each song is about 30 seconds long.

We will use the Python library, `librosa` to extract features from the songs. We will use **Mel-frequency cepstral coefficients (MFCC)**. MFCC values mimic human hearing and they are commonly used in speech recognition applications as well as music genre detection. These MFCC values will be fed directly into the neural network.

To help us understand the MFCC, let's use two examples. Download Kick Loop 5 by Stereo Surgeon. You can do this by visiting `https://freesound.org/people/Stereo%20Surgeon/sounds/266093/`, and download Whistling by cmagar by visiting `https://freesound.org/people/grrlrighter/sounds/98195/`. One of them is a low-bass beat and the other is a higher pitched whistling. They are clearly different and we are going to see how they look different with MFCC values.

Let's go to the code. First, we have to import the `librosa` library. We will also import `glob` because we are going to list the files in the different genre directories. Also, import `numpy` as usual. We will import `matplotlib` to draw the MFCC graphs. Then, will import the Sequential model from Keras. This is a typical feed-forward neural network. Finally, we will import the dense neural network layer, which is just a layer that has a bunch of neurons in it:

```
In [1]: import librosa
        import librosa.feature
        import librosa.display
        import glob
        import numpy as np
        import matplotlib.pyplot as plt
        from keras.models import Sequential
        from keras.layers import Dense, Activation
        from keras.utils.np_utils import to_categorical

        Using TensorFlow backend.
```

Unlike a convolution, for example, it's going to have 2D representations. We are going to use import activation, which allows us to give each neuron layer an activation function, and we will also import `to_categorical`, which allows us to turn the class names into things such as rock, disco, and so forth, which is what's called one-hot encoding.

We have officially developed a helper function to display the MFCC values:

```
In [2]: def display_mfcc(song):
            y, _ = librosa.load(song)
            mfcc = librosa.feature.mfcc(y)

            plt.figure(figsize=(10, 4))
            librosa.display.specshow(mfcc, x_axis='time', y_axis='mel')
            plt.colorbar()
            plt.title(song)
            plt.tight_layout()
            plt.show()
```

First, we will load the song and then extract the MFCC values from it. Then, we'll use the `specshow`, which is a spectrogram show from the `librosa` library.

Here's the kick drum:

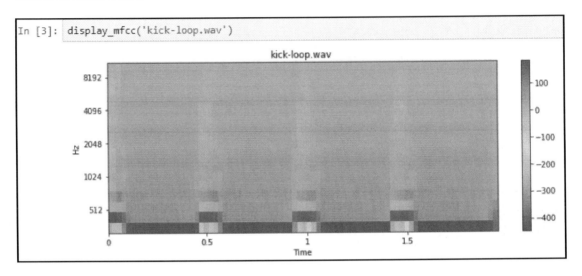

We can see that at low frequency, the bass is very obvious and the rest of the time it's kind of like a wash. Not many other frequencies are represented.

However, if we look at the whistling, it's pretty clear that there's higher frequencies being represented:

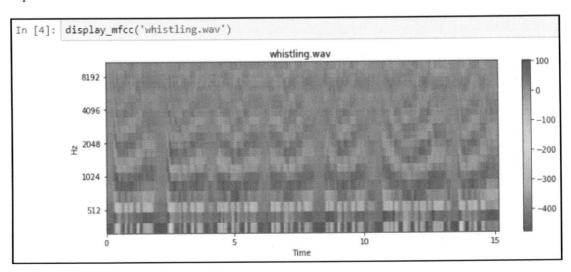

The darker the color, or closer to red, the more power is in that frequency range at that time. So, you can even see the kind of change in frequency with the whistles.

Now, here is the frequency for disco songs:

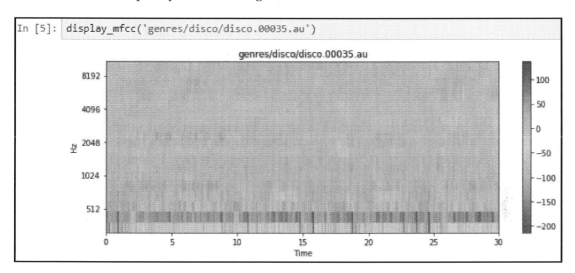

This is the frequency output:

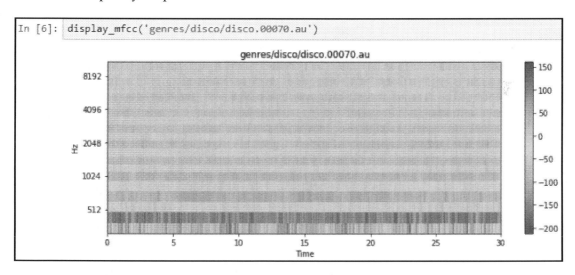

You can sort of see the beats in the preceding outputs, but they're only 30 seconds long, so it is a little bit hard to see the individual beats.

Compare this with classical where there are not so much beats as a continuous kind of bassline such as one that would come from a cello, for example:

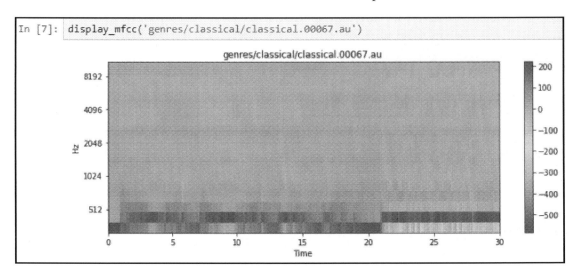

Here is the frequency for hip-hop songs:

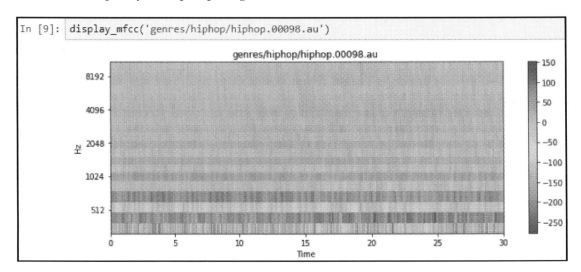

```
In [10]: display_mfcc('genres/hiphop/hiphop.00028.au')
```

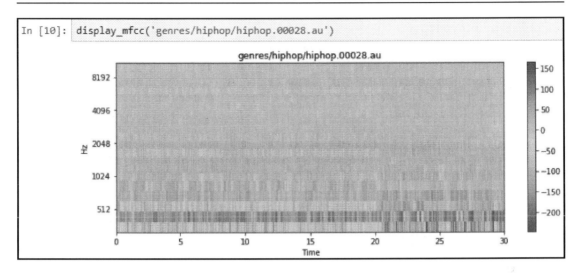

It looks kind of similar to disco, but if it were required that we could tell the difference with our own eyes, we wouldn't really need a neural network because it'd probably be a relatively simple problem. So, the fact that we can't really tell the difference between these is not our problem, it's the neural network's problem.

We have another auxiliary function here that again just loads the MFCC values, but this time we are preparing it for the neural network:

```
In [11]: def extract_features_song(f):
             y, _ = librosa.load(f)

             # get Mel-frequency cepstral coefficients
             mfcc = librosa.feature.mfcc(y)
             # normalize values between -1,1 (divide by max)
             mfcc /= np.amax(np.absolute(mfcc))

             return np.ndarray.flatten(mfcc)[:25000]
```

We have loaded the MFCC values for the song, but because these values are between maybe negative 250 to positive 150, they are no good for a neural network. We don't want to feed in these large and small values. We want to feed in values near negative 1 and positive 1 or from 0 to 1. Therefore, we are going to figure out what the max is, the absolute value for each song, and then divide all the values by that max. Also, the songs are a slightly different length, so we want to pick just 25,000 MFCC values. We have to be super certain that what we feed into the neural network is always the same size, because there are only so many input neurons and we can't change that once we've built the network.

Next, we have a function called `generate _features_and_labels`, which will go through all the different genres and go through all the songs in the dataset and produce those MFCC values and the class names:

```
In [12]:  def generate_features_and_labels():
              all_features = []
              all_labels = []

              genres = ['blues', 'classical', 'country', 'disco', 'hiphop', 'jazz', 'metal', 'pop', 'reggae', 'rock']
              for genre in genres:
                  sound_files = glob.glob('genres/'+genre+'/*.au')
                  print('Processing %d songs in %s genre...' % (len(sound_files), genre))
                  for f in sound_files:
                      features = extract_features_song(f)
                      all_features.append(features)
                      all_labels.append(genre)

              # convert labels to one-hot encoding
              label_uniq_ids, label_row_ids = np.unique(all_labels, return_inverse=True)
              label_row_ids = label_row_ids.astype(np.int32, copy=False)
              onehot_labels = to_categorical(label_row_ids, len(label_uniq_ids))
              return np.stack(all_features), onehot_labels
```

As shown in the preceding screenshot, we will prepare a list for all the features and all the labels. Go through each of the 10 genres. For each genre, we will look at the files in that folder. The `'generes/'+genre+'/*.au'` folder shows how the dataset is organized. When we are processing that folder, there will be 100 songs each for each file, we will extract the features and put those features in the `all_features.append(features)` list. The name of the genre for that song needs to be put in a list also. So, at the end, all features will have 1,000 entries and all labels will have 1,000 entries. In the case of all features, each of those 1,000 entries will have 25,000 entries. That will be a 1,000 x 25,000 matrix.

For all labels at the moment, there is a 1,000 entry-long list, and inside are words such as `blues`, `classical`, `country`, `disco`, `hiphop`, `jazz`, `metal`, `pop`, `reggae`, and `rock`. Now, this is going to be a problem because a neural network is not going to predict a word or even letters. We need to give it a one-hot encoding, which means that each word here is going to be represented as ten binary numbers. In the case of the blues, it is going to be one and then nine zeros. In the case of classical, it is going to be zero followed by one, followed by nine zeros, and so forth. First, we have to figure out all the unique names by using the `np.unique(all_labels, return_inverse=True)` command to get them back as integers. Then, we have to use `to_categorical`, which turns those integers into one-hot encoding. So, what comes back is 1000 x 10 dimensions. 1,000 because there are 1,000 songs, and each of those has ten binary numbers to represent the one-hot encoding. Then, return all the features stacked together by the command return `np.stack(all_features)`, `onehot_labels` into a single matrix, as well as the one-hot matrix. So, we will call that upper function and save the features and labels:

```
In [13]:  features, labels = generate_features_and_labels()

          Processing 100 songs in blues genre...
          Processing 100 songs in classical genre...
          Processing 100 songs in country genre...
          Processing 100 songs in disco genre...
          Processing 100 songs in hiphop genre...
          Processing 100 songs in jazz genre...
          Processing 100 songs in metal genre...
          Processing 100 songs in pop genre...
          Processing 100 songs in reggae genre...
          Processing 100 songs in rock genre...
```

Just to be sure, we will print the shape of the features and the labels as shown in the following screenshot. So, it is 1,000 by 25,000 for the features and 1,000 by 10 for the labels. Now, we will split the dataset into a train and test split. Let's decide the 80% mark defined as training_split= 0.8 to perform a split:

```
In [14]:  print(np.shape(features))
          print(np.shape(labels))

          training_split = 0.8

          # last column has genre, turn it into unique ids
          alldata = np.column_stack((features, labels))

          np.random.shuffle(alldata)
          splitidx = int(len(alldata) * training_split)
          train, test = alldata[:splitidx,:], alldata[splitidx:,:]

          print(np.shape(train))
          print(np.shape(test))

          train_input = train[:,:-10]
          train_labels = train[:,-10:]

          test_input = test[:,:-10]
          test_labels = test[:,-10:]

          print(np.shape(train_input))
          print(np.shape(train_labels))

          (1000, 25000)
          (1000, 10)
          (800, 25010)
          (200, 25010)
          (800, 25000)
          (800, 10)
```

Before that, we will shuffle, and before we shuffle, we need to put the labels with the features so that they don't shuffle in different orders. We will call `np.random.shuffle(alldata)` and do the shuffle, split it using `splitidx=int(len(alldata)*training_split)`, and then we will have train and testsets, as shown in the snapshot earlier. Looking at the shape of the train and the testsets, the train is 800, so 80% of the 1,000 for the rows: we have 25,010 features. Those aren't really all features, though. It is actually the 25,000 features plus the 10 for the one-hot encoding because, remember, we stacked those together before we shuffled. Therefore, we're going to have to strip that back off. We can do that with `train_input = train[:, :-10]`. For both the train input and the test input, we take everything but the last 10 columns, and for the labels, we take the 10 columns to the end, and then we can see what the shapes of the train input and train labels are. So now, we have the proper 800 by 25,000 and 800 by 10.

Next, we'll build the neural network:

```
In [15]:  model = Sequential([
              Dense(100, input_dim=np.shape(train_input)[1]),
              Activation('relu'),
              Dense(10),
              Activation('softmax'),
              ])

          model.compile(optimizer='adam',
                      loss='categorical_crossentropy',
                      metrics=['accuracy'])
          print(model.summary())

          model.fit(train_input, train_labels, epochs=10, batch_size=32,
                  validation_split=0.2)

          loss, acc = model.evaluate(test_input, test_labels, batch_size=32)

          print("Done!")
          print("Loss: %.4f, accuracy: %.4f" % (loss, acc))
```

We are going to have a sequential neural network. The first layer will be a dense layers of 100 neurons. Now, just on the first layer, it matters that you give the input dimensions or the input shape, and that's going to be 25,000 in our case. This says how many input values are coming per example. Those 25,000 are going to connect to the 100 in the first layer. The first layer will do its weighted sum of its inputs, its weights, and bias term, and then we are going to run the `relu` activation function. `relu`, if you recall, states that anything less than 0 will turn out to be a 0. Anything higher than 0 will just be the value itself. These 100 will then connect to 10 more and that will be the output layer. It will be 10 because we have done someone-hot encoding and we have 10 binary numbers in that encoding.

The activation used in the code, `softmax`, says to take the output of the 10 and normalize them so that they add up to 1. That way, they end up being probabilities and whichever one of the 10 is the highest scoring, the highest probability, we take that to be the prediction and that will directly correspond to whichever position that highest number is in. For example, if it is in position 4, that would be disco (look in the code).

Next, we will compile the model, choose an optimizer such as Adam, and define the `loss` function. Any time you have multiple outputs like we have here (we have 10), you probably want to do categorical cross-entropy and metrics accuracy to see the accuracy as it's training and during evaluation, in addition to the loss, which is always shown: however, accuracy makes more sense to us. Next, we can print `model.summary`, which tells us details about the layers.

It will look something like the following:

```
Layer (type)                 Output Shape              Param #
=================================================================
dense_1 (Dense)              (None, 100)               2500100
_____
activation_1 (Activation)    (None, 100)               0
_____
dense_2 (Dense)              (None, 10)                1010
_____
activation_2 (Activation)    (None, 10)                0
=================================================================
Total params: 2,501,110
Trainable params: 2,501,110
Non-trainable params: 0
_____
None
```

The output shape of the first 100 neuron layer is definitely 100 values because there are 100 neurons, and the output of the dense second layer is 10 because there are 10 neurons. So, why are there 2.5 million parameters, or weights, in the first layer? That's because we have 25,000 inputs. Well, we have 25,000 inputs and each one of those inputs is going to each one of the 100 dense neurons. So that's 2.5 million, and then plus 100, because each of those neurons in the 100 has its own bias term, its own bias weight, and that needs to be learned as well.

Overall, we have about 2.5 million parameters or weights. Next, we run the fit. It takes the training input and training labels, and takes the number of epochs that we want. We want 10, so that's 10 repeats over the trained input; it takes a batch size which says how many, in our case, songs to go through before updating the weights; and a `validation_split` of 0.2 says *take 20% of that trained input, split it out, don't actually train on that, and use that to evaluate how well it's doing after every epoch*. It never actually trains on the validation split, but the validation split lets us look at the progress as it goes.

Finally, because we did separate the training and test ahead of time, we're going to do an evaluation on the test, the test data, and print the loss and accuracy of that. Here it is with the training results:

```
Train on 640 samples, validate on 160 samples
Epoch 1/10
640/640 [==============================] - 2s 3ms/step - loss: 2.0585 - acc: 0.2906 - val_loss: 1.7780 - val_acc: 0.3187
Epoch 2/10
640/640 [==============================] - 0s 720us/step - loss: 1.4080 - acc: 0.5031 - val_loss: 1.5680 - val_acc: 0.4562
Epoch 3/10
640/640 [==============================] - 0s 723us/step - loss: 1.1128 - acc: 0.6281 - val_loss: 1.5202 - val_acc: 0.4625
Epoch 4/10
640/640 [==============================] - 0s 697us/step - loss: 0.8968 - acc: 0.7422 - val_loss: 1.4163 - val_acc: 0.5062
Epoch 5/10
640/640 [==============================] - 0s 707us/step - loss: 0.7990 - acc: 0.7734 - val_loss: 1.9091 - val_acc: 0.4625
Epoch 6/10
640/640 [==============================] - 0s 712us/step - loss: 0.6336 - acc: 0.8266 - val_loss: 1.4158 - val_acc: 0.5375
Epoch 7/10
640/640 [==============================] - 0s 690us/step - loss: 0.4935 - acc: 0.9031 - val_loss: 1.4425 - val_acc: 0.5188
Epoch 8/10
640/640 [==============================] - 0s 717us/step - loss: 0.3547 - acc: 0.9500 - val_loss: 1.4821 - val_acc: 0.4813
Epoch 9/10
640/640 [==============================] - 0s 710us/step - loss: 0.2855 - acc: 0.9672 - val_loss: 1.4005 - val_acc: 0.5312
Epoch 10/10
640/640 [==============================] - 0s 706us/step - loss: 0.2247 - acc: 0.9891 - val_loss: 1.4223 - val_acc: 0.4938
200/200 [==============================] - 0s 452us/step
Done!
Loss: 1.5206, accuracy: 0.5250
```

It was printing this as it went. It always prints the loss and the accuracy. This is on the training set itself, not the validation set, so this should get pretty close to 1.0. You actually probably don't want it to go close to 1.0 because that could represent overfitting, but if you let it go long enough, it often does reach 1.0 accuracy on the training set because it's memorizing the training set. What we really care about is the validation accuracy because that's letting us use the test set. It's data that it's just never looked at before, at least not for training, and indeed it's relatively close to the validation accuracy, which is our final accuracy. This final accuracy is on the test data that we separated ahead of time. Now we're getting an accuracy of around 53%. That seems relatively low until we realize that there are 10 different genres. Random guessing would give us 10% accuracy, so it's a lot better than random guessing.

Revising the spam detector to use neural networks

In this section, we're going to update the spam detector from before to use neural networks. Recall that the dataset used was from YouTube. There was an approximate of 2,000 comments with around half being spam and the other half not. These comments were of five different videos.

In the last version, we used a bag of words and a random forest. We carried out a parameter search to find the parameters best suited for the bag of words, which was the CountVectorizer that had 1,000 different words in it. These 1000 words were the top used words. We used unigrams instead of bigrams or trigrams. It would be good to drop the common and the stop words from the English language. The best way is to use TF-IDF. It was also found that using a 100 different trees would be best for the random forest. Now, we are going to use a bag of words but we're going to use a shallow neural network instead of the random forest. Also remember that we got 95 or 96 percent accuracy for the previous version.

Let's look at the code:

```
In [28]:  import pandas as pd
          from keras.preprocessing.text import Tokenizer
          import numpy as np
          from keras.models import Sequential
          from keras.layers import Dense, Dropout, Activation
          from keras.utils import np_utils
          from sklearn.model_selection import StratifiedKFold
```

We start with importing. We'll use pandas once more to load the dataset. This time, we're going to use the Keras Tokenizer. There's no particular reason to use Tokenizer, except to show an alternative technique. We will import NumPy and then proceed to import the sequential model for the neural networks, which is the typical feed-forward network. We then have dense layers that are the typical neuron layers. We're also going to add the dropout feature, which helps prevent over-fitting, and we're going to decide on the activation for each layer. We are going to use the `to_categorical` method from the `np_utils` library from Keras to produce one-hot encoding, and we're going to introduce `StratifiedKFold` to perform our cross-validation.

First, we load the datasets:

```
In [29]:  d = pd.concat([pd.read_csv("Youtube01-Psy.csv"),
                         pd.read_csv("Youtube02-KatyPerry.csv"),
                         pd.read_csv("Youtube03-LMFAO.csv"),
                         pd.read_csv("Youtube04-Eminem.csv"),
                         pd.read_csv("Youtube05-Shakira.csv")])
          d = d.sample(frac=1)
```

There are five different CSV files. We will stack them on top of each other so that we have one big dataset. We then shuffle it by running a sample which picks random rows. We're going to say that we want to keep 100% of the data so that it effectively shuffles all of the data.

Now, the `StratifiedKFold` technique takes a number of splits, say five, and produces the indexes of the original dataset for those splits:

```
In [30]:   kfold = StratifiedKFold(n_splits=5)
           splits = kfold.split(d, d['CLASS'])
```

We're going to get an 80%/20% split for training and testing. This 20% testing will differ with each split. It's an iterator, hence, we can use a `for` loop to look at all the different splits. We will print the testing positions to see that they don't overlap for each split:

```
In [31]:   for train, test in splits:
             |   print("Split")
                 print(test)
```

Here's the first split:

```
Split
[   0   1   2   3   4   5   6   7   8   9  10  11  12  13  14  15  16  17
   18  19  20  21  22  23  24  25  26  27  28  29  30  31  32  33  34  35
   36  37  38  39  40  41  42  43  44  45  46  47  48  49  50  51  52  53
   54  55  56  57  58  59  60  61  62  63  64  65  66  67  68  69  70  71
   72  73  74  75  76  77  78  79  80  81  82  83  84  85  86  87  88  89
   90  91  92  93  94  95  96  97  98  99 100 101 102 103 104 105 106 107
  108 109 110 111 112 113 114 115 116 117 118 119 120 121 122 123 124 125
  126 127 128 129 130 131 132 133 134 135 136 137 138 139 140 141 142 143
  144 145 146 147 148 149 150 151 152 153 154 155 156 157 158 159 160 161
  162 163 164 165 166 167 168 169 170 171 172 173 174 175 176 177 178 179
  180 181 182 183 184 185 186 187 188 189 190 191 192 193 194 195 196 197
  198 199 200 201 202 203 204 205 206 207 208 209 210 211 212 213 214 215
  216 217 218 219 220 221 222 223 224 225 226 227 228 229 230 231 232 233
  234 235 236 237 238 239 240 241 242 243 244 245 246 247 248 249 250 251
  252 253 254 255 256 257 258 259 260 261 262 263 264 265 266 267 268 269
  270 271 272 273 274 275 276 277 278 279 280 281 282 283 284 285 286 287
  288 289 290 291 292 293 294 295 296 297 298 299 300 301 302 303 304 305
  306 307 308 309 310 311 312 313 314 315 316 317 318 319 320 321 322 323
```

Here's the second split:

```
Split
[385 393 394 395 396 397 398 399 400 401 402 403 404 405 406 407 408 409
 410 411 412 413 414 415 416 417 418 419 420 421 422 423 424 425 426 427
 428 429 430 431 432 433 434 435 436 437 438 439 440 441 442 443 444 445
 446 447 448 449 450 451 452 453 454 455 456 457 458 459 460 461 462 463
 464 465 466 467 468 469 470 471 472 473 474 475 476 477 478 479 480 481
 482 483 484 485 486 487 488 489 490 491 492 493 494 495 496 497 498 499
 500 501 502 503 504 505 506 507 508 509 510 511 512 513 514 515 516 517
 518 519 520 521 522 523 524 525 526 527 528 529 530 531 532 533 534 535
 536 537 538 539 540 541 542 543 544 545 546 547 548 549 550 551 552 553
 554 555 556 557 558 559 560 561 562 563 564 565 566 567 568 569 570 571
 572 573 574 575 576 577 578 579 580 581 582 583 584 585 586 587 588 589
 590 591 592 593 594 595 596 597 598 599 600 601 602 603 604 605 606 607
 608 609 610 611 612 613 614 615 616 617 618 619 620 621 622 623 624 625
 626 627 628 629 630 631 632 633 634 635 636 637 638 639 640 641 642 643
 644 645 646 647 648 649 650 651 652 653 654 655 656 657 658 659 660 661
 662 663 664 665 666 667 668 669 670 671 672 673 674 675 676 677 678 679
 680 681 682 683 684 685 686 687 688 689 690 691 692 693 694 695 696 697
 698 699 700 701 702 703 704 705 706 707 708 709 710 711 712 713 714 715
```

Here's the third:

```
Split
[ 757  759  761  763  765  771  772  773  776  777  781  783  784  787  789
  791  793  794  796  798  799  801  802  803  804  807  808  810  811  812
  813  814  815  816  817  818  819  820  821  822  823  824  825  826  827
  828  829  830  831  832  833  834  835  836  837  838  839  840  841  842
  843  844  845  846  847  848  849  850  851  852  853  854  855  856  857
  858  859  860  861  862  863  864  865  866  867  868  869  870  871  872
  873  874  875  876  877  878  879  880  881  882  883  884  885  886  887
  888  889  890  891  892  893  894  895  896  897  898  899  900  901  902
  903  904  905  906  907  908  909  910  911  912  913  914  915  916  917
  918  919  920  921  922  923  924  925  926  927  928  929  930  931  932
  933  934  935  936  937  938  939  940  941  942  943  944  945  946  947
  948  949  950  951  952  953  954  955  956  957  958  959  960  961  962
  963  964  965  966  967  968  969  970  971  972  973  974  975  976  977
  978  979  980  981  982  983  984  985  986  987  988  989  990  991  992
  993  994  995  996  997  998  999 1000 1001 1002 1003 1004 1005 1006 1007
 1008 1009 1010 1011 1012 1013 1014 1015 1016 1017 1018 1019 1020 1021 1022
 1023 1024 1025 1026 1027 1028 1029 1030 1031 1032 1033 1034 1035 1036 1037
```

Here's the fourth:

```
Split
[1136 1139 1140 1143 1144 1147 1148 1150 1151 1153 1158 1160 1166 1167 1169
 1171 1172 1176 1180 1181 1184 1187 1190 1192 1194 1198 1200 1201 1202 1203
 1204 1205 1206 1207 1208 1209 1210 1211 1212 1213 1214 1215 1216 1217 1218
 1219 1220 1221 1222 1223 1224 1225 1226 1227 1228 1229 1230 1231 1232 1233
 1234 1235 1236 1237 1238 1239 1240 1241 1242 1243 1244 1245 1246 1247 1248
 1249 1250 1251 1252 1253 1254 1255 1256 1257 1258 1259 1260 1261 1262 1263
 1264 1265 1266 1267 1268 1269 1270 1271 1272 1273 1274 1275 1276 1277 1278
 1279 1280 1281 1282 1283 1284 1285 1286 1287 1288 1289 1290 1291 1292 1293
 1294 1295 1296 1297 1298 1299 1300 1301 1302 1303 1304 1305 1306 1307 1308
 1309 1310 1311 1312 1313 1314 1315 1316 1317 1318 1319 1320 1321 1322 1323
 1324 1325 1326 1327 1328 1329 1330 1331 1332 1333 1334 1335 1336 1337 1338
 1339 1340 1341 1342 1343 1344 1345 1346 1347 1348 1349 1350 1351 1352 1353
 1354 1355 1356 1357 1358 1359 1360 1361 1362 1363 1364 1365 1366 1367 1368
 1369 1370 1371 1372 1373 1374 1375 1376 1377 1378 1379 1380 1381 1382 1383
 1384 1385 1386 1387 1388 1389 1390 1391 1392 1393 1394 1395 1396 1397 1398
 1399 1400 1401 1402 1403 1404 1405 1406 1407 1408 1409 1410 1411 1412 1413
```

And finally, the fifth:

```
Split
[1548 1551 1552 1555 1561 1566 1569 1572 1573 1574 1575 1576 1577 1578 1579
 1580 1581 1582 1583 1584 1585 1586 1587 1588 1589 1590 1591 1592 1593 1594
 1595 1596 1597 1598 1599 1600 1601 1602 1603 1604 1605 1606 1607 1608 1609
 1610 1611 1612 1613 1614 1615 1616 1617 1618 1619 1620 1621 1622 1623 1624
 1625 1626 1627 1628 1629 1630 1631 1632 1633 1634 1635 1636 1637 1638 1639
 1640 1641 1642 1643 1644 1645 1646 1647 1648 1649 1650 1651 1652 1653 1654
 1655 1656 1657 1658 1659 1660 1661 1662 1663 1664 1665 1666 1667 1668 1669
 1670 1671 1672 1673 1674 1675 1676 1677 1678 1679 1680 1681 1682 1683 1684
 1685 1686 1687 1688 1689 1690 1691 1692 1693 1694 1695 1696 1697 1698 1699
 1700 1701 1702 1703 1704 1705 1706 1707 1708 1709 1710 1711 1712 1713 1714
 1715 1716 1717 1718 1719 1720 1721 1722 1723 1724 1725 1726 1727 1728 1729
 1730 1731 1732 1733 1734 1735 1736 1737 1738 1739 1740 1741 1742 1743 1744
 1745 1746 1747 1748 1749 1750 1751 1752 1753 1754 1755 1756 1757 1758 1759
 1760 1761 1762 1763 1764 1765 1766 1767 1768 1769 1770 1771 1772 1773 1774
 1775 1776 1777 1778 1779 1780 1781 1782 1783 1784 1785 1786 1787 1788 1789
```

It is now obvious that they don't overlap.

We then define a function that receives these indexes for the different splits and does the bag of words, builds a neural net, trains it, and evaluates it. We then return the score for that split. We begin by taking the positions for the train and test sets and extract the comments:

```
In [41]: def train_and_test(train_idx, test_idx):

             train_content = d['CONTENT'].iloc[train_idx]
             test_content = d['CONTENT'].iloc[test_idx]

             tokenizer = Tokenizer(num_words=2000)

             # learn the training words (not the testing words!)
             tokenizer.fit_on_texts(train_content)

             # options for mode: binary, freq, tfidf
             d_train_inputs = tokenizer.texts_to_matrix(train_content, mode='tfidf')
             d_test_inputs = tokenizer.texts_to_matrix(test_content, mode='tfidf')

             # divide tfidf by max
             d_train_inputs = d_train_inputs/np.amax(np.absolute(d_train_inputs))
             d_test_inputs = d_test_inputs/np.amax(np.absolute(d_test_inputs))

             # subtract mean, to get values between -1 and 1
             d_train_inputs = d_train_inputs - np.mean(d_train_inputs)
             d_test_inputs = d_test_inputs - np.mean(d_test_inputs)
```

We then proceed to build our Tokenizer. At this point, we can mention the number of words we want it to support in the Tokenizer. A general research led us to the conclusion that using 2,000 words was better than a 1000 words. For the random forest, using a 1,000 words is better and is supported by doing the GridSearch for all the different parameters. There's no particular reason to believe that because the bag of words works best with a 1,000 words in comparison to the random forest, that it is what is necessarily best for the neural network as well. So, we're going to use 2,000 words in this case. This is just a constructor. Nothing has really happened with the bag of words yet. The next thing we need to do is learn what the words are and that's going to happen by using the `fit_on_texts` method.

Now, `fit_on_texts` should only be used on the training set. We only want to learn the words in the training set. This helps us simulate the real world where you've only trained your model on a certain set of data and then the real world presents possibly something new that you've never seen before. To do this, we have a training testing split. We only want to learn the words on the training set. If there are words in the testing set that we've never seen before in the training set, they'll be ignored. This is good because that's how it's going to work in the real world.

We'll learn the words on the training set but then transform both the training and the testing comments into the bag of words model. The `texts_to _matrix` is used for the same. It produces a matrix which can be fed directly into the neural network. We give it the `train_content`, which are the comments, and the `test_content`. Then, we can then decide if we want `tfidf` scores, binary scores, or frequency counts. We're going to go with `tfidf` in this case. `tfidf` is a number between 0 and any random integer, possibly a large number, and in most cases it's not a good idea to give a neuron in a neural network very large numbers or very small numbers, meaning negative numbers. Here, we want to kind of scale these numbers between maybe 0 and 1, and -1 and 1. To scale between 0 and 1, we can divide by the max. So, we have to look at all the training examples, all the training numbers for TF-IDF, and divide each number by the maximum among those. We have to do the same for the test. Now, the train inputs and test inputs are `tfidf` scores that have been rescaled to 0 to 1.

We also shift it between -1 and 1 by subtracting the average from each score. Now, for the outputs, even though we could use binary, we're going to use categorical in this case for no particular reason, except just to show it. We're going to take all of the desired outputs, the classes, which is spam, not spam, and turn them into 1, 0 and 0, 1 encodings.

Now, we can build our network. We're going to build the network all over again for each train/test split so it starts randomly. We're going to build a sequential network, which is a typical feed-forward network. We're going to have a first layer of 512 neurons. They're going to receive 2,000 different inputs. There's 2,000 because that's the size of the bag of words.

We then use a ReLU activation. We could also use Tanh. ReLU is common in neural networks today. It's pretty fast as well as accurate. There's a 512 layer and then a 2 layer. The 2 is very specific because that's the output. We have one-hot encoding, so it's 1, 0, 0, 1, so that's two neurons. It has to match the number of outputs we have. Each of the two has links to 512 neurons from before. That's a lot of edges connecting the first layer to the second layer.

To prevent overfitting, we add a dropout. A 50% dropout means that every time it goes to update the weights, it just refuses to update half of them, a random half. We then find the weighted sum of their inputs.

We take that sum and run the softmax. Softmax takes these different outputs and turns them into probabilities so that one of them is highest and they're all between 0 and 1. Then, we compile the model to compute the loss as `categorical_ crossentropy`. This is usually something one uses when they use one-hot encoding. Let's use the Adamax optimizer. There are different optimizers that are available in Keras, and you can look at the Keras documentation at `https://keras.io/`.

Accuracy is an essential measure to work on while we train the network, and we also want to compute accuracy at the very end to see how well it's done.

We then run fit on the training set. `d_train_inputs` is the train inputs, and `d_train_inputs` is the matrix bag of words model, train outputs, and the one -hot encoding. We are going to say that we want 10 epochs, which means it'll go through the entire training set ten times, and a batch size of 16, which means it will go through 16 rows and compute the average loss and then update the weight.

After it's been fit, which indirectly means it's been trained, we evaluate the test. It's not until this point that it actually looks at the test. The scores that come out are going to be the loss and whatever other metrics we have, which in this case is accuracy. Therefore, we'll just show the accuracy times 100 to get a percent and we'll return the scores.

Now, let's build that split again, which is the k-fold split with five different folds:

```
In [42]:  kfold = StratifiedKFold(n_splits=5)
          splits = kfold.split(d, d['CLASS'])
          cvscores = []
          for train_idx, test_idx, in splits:
              scores = train_and_test(train_idx, test_idx)
              cvscores.append(scores[1] * 100)

Epoch 1/10
1564/1564 [==============================] - 3s 2ms/step - loss: 0.5992 - acc: 0.7986
Epoch 2/10
1564/1564 [==============================] - 1s 582us/step - loss: 0.3709 - acc: 0.9137
Epoch 3/10
1564/1564 [==============================] - 1s 582us/step - loss: 0.2382 - acc: 0.9425
Epoch 4/10
1564/1564 [==============================] - 1s 581us/step - loss: 0.1761 - acc: 0.9520
Epoch 5/10
1564/1564 [==============================] - 1s 575us/step - loss: 0.1457 - acc: 0.9584
```

We collect the scores. For each split, we're going to run our `train_and_test` function and save the scores. Here, it is running on each split. If you scroll, you will see that you get the epochs going. We can see that the accuracy on the training input increases per epoch. Now, if this gets really high, you might start worrying about over-fitting, but after the 10 epochs, use the testing set which it's never seen before. This helps us obtain the accuracy number for the testing set. Then, we'll do it all again for the next split and we'll get a different accuracy. We'll do this a few more times until we have five different numbers, one for each split.

The average is found as follows: :

```
In [43]:  print("%.2f%% (+/- %.2f%%)" % (np.mean(cvscores), np.std(cvscores)))

          95.09% (+/- 1.72%)
```

Here, we get 95%, which is very close to what we got by using random forest. We didn't use this neural network example to show that we can get 100%. We used this method to demonstrate an alternative way to detect spam instead of the random forest method.

Summary

In this chapter, we covered a brief introduction to neural networks, proceeded with feed-forward neural networks, and looked at a program to identify the genre of a song with neural networks. Finally, we revised our spam detector from earlier to make it work with neural networks.

In the next chapter, we'll look at deep learning and learn about convolutional neural networks.

5
Deep Learning

In this chapter, we'll cover some of the basics of deep learning. Deep learning refers to neural networks with lots of layers. It's kind of a buzzword, but the technology behind it is real and quite sophisticated.

The term has been rising in popularity along with machine learning and artificial intelligence, as shown in this Google trend chart:

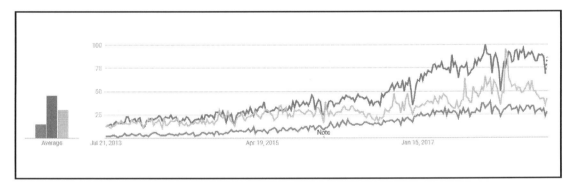

As stated by some of the inventors of deep learning methods, the primary advantage of deep learning is that adding more data and more computing power often produces more accurate results, without the significant effort required for engineering.

In this chapter, we are going to be looking at the following:

- Deep learning methods
- Identifying handwritten mathematical symbols with CNNs
- Revisiting the bird species identifier to use images

Deep learning methods

Deep learning refers to several methods which may be used in a particular application. These methods include convolutional layers and pooling. Simpler and faster activation functions, such as ReLU, return the neuron's weighted sum if it's positive and zero if negative. Regularization techniques, such as dropout, randomly ignore weights during the weight update base to prevent overfitting. GPUs are used for faster training with the order that is 50 times faster. This is because they're optimized for matrix calculations that are used extensively in neural networks and memory units for applications such as speech recognition.

Several factors have contributed to deep learning's dramatic growth in the last five years. Large public datasets, such as ImageNet, that holds millions of labeled images covering a thousand categories and Mozilla's Common Voice Project, that contain speech samples are now available. Such datasets have satisfied the basic requirement for deep learning-lot of training data. GPUs have transitioned to deep learning and clusters while also focusing on gaming. This helps make large-scale deep learning possible.

Advanced software frameworks that were released open source and are undergoing rapid improvement are also available to everyone. These include TensorFlow, Keras, Torch, and Caffe. Deep architectures that achieve state-of-the-art results, such as Inception-v3 are being used for the ImageNet dataset. This network actually has an approximate of 24 million parameters, and a large community of researchers and software engineers quickly translating research prototypes into open source software that anyone can download, evaluate, and extend.

Convolutions and pooling

This sections takes a closer look at two fundamental deep learning technologies, namely, convolution and pooling. Throughout this section, we will be using images to understand these concepts. Nevertheless, what we'll be studying can also be applied to other data, such as, audio signals. Let's take a look at the following photo and begin by zooming in to observe the pixels:

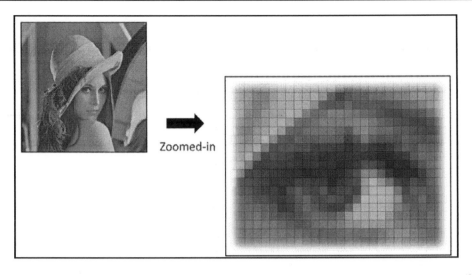

Convolutions occur per channel. An input image would generally consist of three channels; red, green, and blue. The next step would be to separate these three colors. The following diagram depicts this:

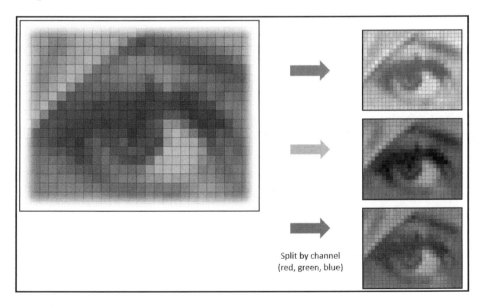

A convolution is a kernel. In this image, we apply a 3 x 3 kernel. Every kernel contains a number of weights. The kernel slides around the image and computes the weighted sum of the pixels on the kernel, each multiplied by their corresponding kernel weights:

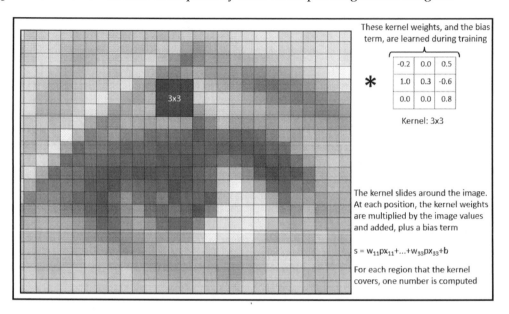

A bias term is also added. A single number, the weighted sum, is produced for each position that the kernel slides over. The kernel's weights start off with any random value and change during the training phase. The following diagram shows three examples of kernels with different weights:

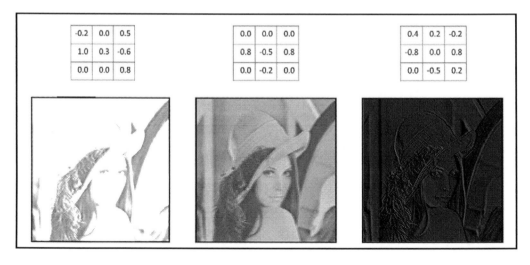

You can see how the image transforms differently depending on the weights. The rightmost image highlights the edges, which is often useful for identifying objects. The stride helps us understand how the kernel slides across the image. The following diagram is an example of a 1 x 1 stride:

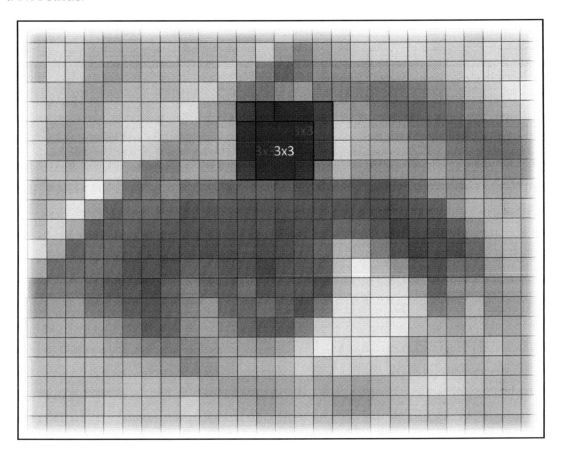

The kernel moves by one pixel to the right and then down. Throughout this process, the center of the kernel will hit every pixel of the image whilst overlapping the other kernels. It is also observed that some pixels are missed by the center of the kernel. The following image depicts a 2 x 2 stride:

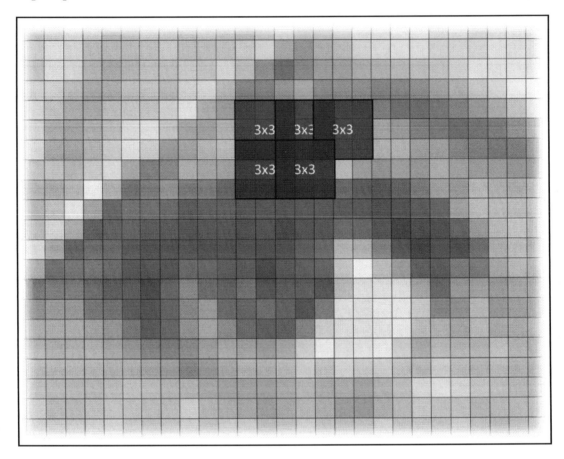

In certain cases, it is observed that no overlapping takes place. To prove this, the following diagram contains a 3 x 3 stride:

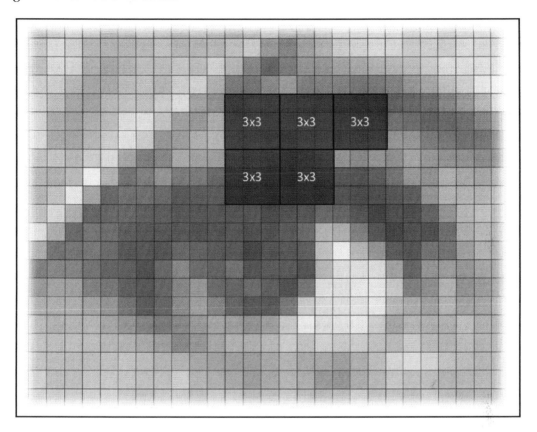

In such cases, no overlap takes place because the kernel is the same size as the stride.

However, the borders of the image need to be handled differently. To affect this, we can use padding. This helps avoid extending the kernel across the border. Padding consists of extra pixels, which are always zero. They don't contribute to the weighted sum. The padding allows the kernel's weights to cover every region of the image while still letting the kernels assume the stride is 1. The kernel produces one output for every region it covers. Hence, if we have a stride that is greater than 1, we'll have fewer outputs than there were original pixels. In other words, the convolution helped reduce the image's dimensions. The formula shown here tells us the dimensions of the output of a convolution:

$$D = 1 + (W - K + 2*P)/S,$$

W = input width, K = kernel size,
P = padding size, S = stride size

For example, if W = 256, K = 3,
P = 1, and S = 3, then the output
dimension is 85x85

It is a general practice to use square images. Kernels and strides are used for simplicity. This helps us focus on only one dimension, which will be the same for the width and height. In the following diagram, a 3 x 3 kernel with a (3, 3) stride is depicted:

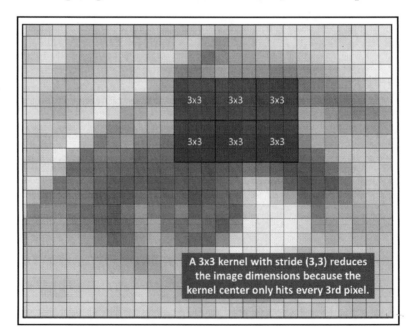

A 3x3 kernel with stride (3,3) reduces the image dimensions because the kernel center only hits every 3rd pixel.

The preceding calculation gives the result of 85 width and 85 height. The image's width and height have effectively been reduced by a factor of three from the original 256. Rather than use a large stride, we shall let the convolution hit every pixel by using a stride of 1. This will help us attain a more practical result. We also need to make sure that there is sufficient padding. However, it is beneficial to reduce the image dimensions as we move through the network. This helps the network train faster as there will be fewer parameters. Fewer parameters imply a smaller chance of over-fitting.

We often use max or average pooling between convolution dimensionality instead of varying the stride length. Pooling looks at a region, which, let us assume, is 2 x 2, and keeps only the largest or average value. The following image depicts a 2 x 2 matrix that depicts pooling:

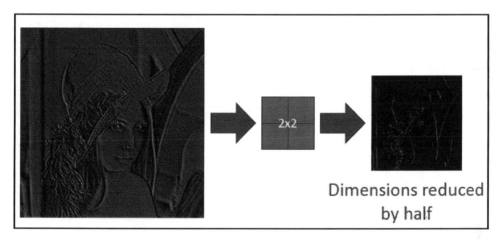

A pooling region always has the same-sized stride as the pool size. This helps avoid overlapping.

Pooling doesn't use any weights, which means there is nothing to train.

Here's a relatively shallow **convolutional neural networks (CNNs)** representation:

We observe that the input image is subjected to various convolutions and pooling layers with ReLU activations between them before finally arriving at a traditionally fully connected network. The fully connected network, though not depicted in the diagram, is ultimately predicting the class. In this example, as in most CNNs, we will have multiple convolutions at each layer. Here, we will observe 10, which are depicted as rows. Each of these 10 convolutions have their own kernels in each column so that different convolutions can be learned at each resolution. The fully connected layers on the right will determine which convolutions best identify the car or the truck, and so forth.

Identifying handwritten mathematical symbols with CNNs

This sections deals with building a CNN to identify handwritten mathematical symbols. We're going to use the HASYv2 dataset. This contains 168,000 images from 369 different classes where each represents a different symbol. This dataset is a more complex analog compared to the popular MNIST dataset, which contains handwritten numbers.

The following diagram depicts the kind of images that are available in this dataset:

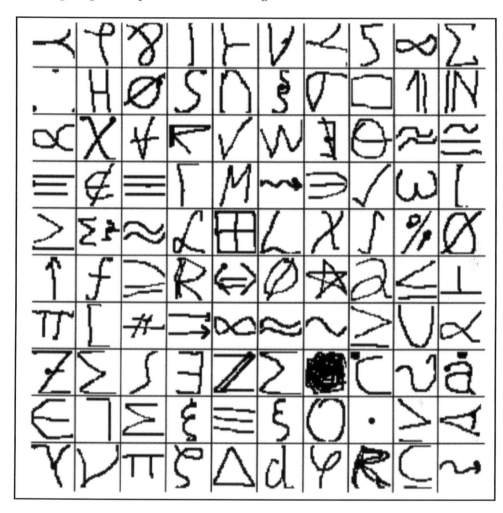

And here, we can see a graph showing how many symbols have different numbers of images:

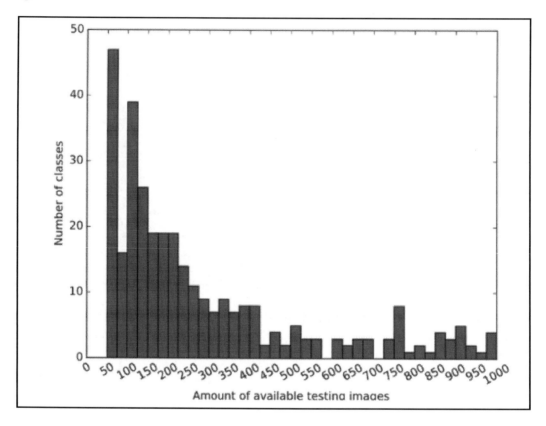

It is observed that many symbols have few images and there are a few that have lots of images. The code to import any image is as follows:

```
In [1]:  from IPython.display import Image
```

We begin by importing the `Image` class from the `IPython` library. This allows us to show images inside Jupyter Notebook. Here's one image from the dataset:

```
In [2]:  # example image from the dataset

         Image(url="HASYv2/hasy-data/v2-00010.png")

Out[2]:  A
```

This is an image of the alphabet **A**. Each image is 30 x 30 pixels. This image is in the RGB format even though it doesn't really need to be RGB. The different channels are predominately black and white or grayscale. We're going to use these three channels. We then proceed to import CSV, which allows us to load the dataset:

```
In [3]:  import csv
         from PIL import Image as pil_image
         import keras.preprocessing.image

         Using TensorFlow backend.
```

This CSV file states all the different filenames and the class names. We import the image class from `pil`, which allows us to load the image. We import `preprocessing.image`, which then allows us to convert the images into `numpy` arrays. Let's us then go through the data file, taking a closer look at every filename and loading it, while recording which class it belongs to:

```
In [4]:  # load all images (as numpy arrays) and save their classes

         imgs = []
         classes = []
         with open('HASYv2/hasy-data-labels.csv') as csvfile:
             csvreader = csv.reader(csvfile)
             i = 0
             for row in csvreader:
                 if i > 0:
                     img = keras.preprocessing.image.img_to_array(pil_image.open("HASYv2/" + row[0]))
                     # neuron activation functions behave best when input values are between 0.0 and 1.0 (or -1.0 and 1.0),
                     # so we rescale each pixel value to be in the range 0.0 to 1.0 instead of 0-255
                     img /= 255.0
                     imgs.append((row[0], row[2], img))
                     classes.append(row[2])
                 i += 1
```

The immediate next step would be to save the images and the classes and use the CSV reader. We need to set a counter to make sure we skip the first row, which is the header of the CSV file. Only after this, we proceed to open the image, which is in the first column of each row. This is converted into an array. The achieved result will have dimensions of 30 x 30 x 3, which is interpreted as 30 width, 30 height, and 3 channels (RGB).

These three channels will have numbers between 0 and 255. These are typical pixel values, which are not good for a neural network. We need values that lie between 0 and 1 or -1 and 1. To do this, we divide each pixel value by 255. To make things easier, we're going to collect the filename, the class name, and the image matrix and put them into our images list. We will also make a note of the name of the class. The following snippet will make us understand the concept to a greater depth:

```
In [5]:  imgs[0]

Out[5]:  ('hasy-data/v2-00000.png', 'A', array([[[ 1.,   1.,   1.],
                [ 1.,   1.,   1.],
                [ 1.,   1.,   1.],
                ...,
                [ 1.,   1.,   1.],
                [ 1.,   1.,   1.],
                [ 1.,   1.,   1.]],

               [[ 1.,   1.,   1.],
                [ 1.,   1.,   1.],
                [ 1.,   1.,   1.],
                ...,
                [ 1.,   1.,   1.],
                [ 1.,   1.,   1.],
                [ 1.,   1.,   1.]],

               [[ 1.,   1.,   1.],
                [ 1.,   1.,   1.],
                [ 1.,   1.,   1.],
                ...,
                [ 1.,   1.,   1.],
                [ 1.,   1.,   1.],
                [ 1.,   1.,   1.]],
```

The file is named `hasy-data/v2-00000.png`. A is the name of the class followed by the array. The array has dimensions 30 x 30 x 3. The innermost and last dimension, is 3. Each **1.0** depicts the color white. We understand this because we divided everything by 255 as mentioned earlier.

We have 168,000 images in the `HASYv2` dataset:

```
In [6]: len(imgs)

Out[6]: 168233
```

We then proceed to shuffle and then split the data on an 80% train, 20% test basis. As seen in the following codeblock, we first shuffle, then proceed to split the image:

```
In [7]: # shuffle the data, split into 80% train, 20% test

import random
random.shuffle(imgs)
split_idx = int(0.8*len(imgs))
train = imgs[:split_idx]
test = imgs[split_idx:]
```

Because we use these tuples with three different values, we're going to need to ultimately collect all that into a matrix:

```
In [8]: import numpy as np

train_input = np.asarray(list(map(lambda row: row[2], train)))
test_input = np.asarray(list(map(lambda row: row[2], test)))

train_output = np.asarray(list(map(lambda row: row[1], train)))
test_output = np.asarray(list(map(lambda row: row[1], test)))
```

We need to collect the images as well as the labels. To collect the images, we go through each row and take each third element. This element is the image matrix. We stick it all together into a `numpy` array. The same is done for the train and test datasets.

For the outputs, we need to go and pick out the second value. These are still strings, such as a and =. We need to convert the second value into one-hot encoding before it can be used for a neural network.

We proceed to use scikit-learn's preprocessing label encoder and one-hot encoder:

```
In [9]:  from sklearn.preprocessing import LabelEncoder
         from sklearn.preprocessing import OneHotEncoder
```

We're going to make a LabelEncoder object and we're going to both fit and transform on the classes:

```
In [10]:  # convert class names into one-hot encoding

          # first, convert class names into integers
          label_encoder = LabelEncoder()
          integer_encoded = label_encoder.fit_transform(classes)

          # then convert integers into one-hot encoding
          onehot_encoder = OneHotEncoder(sparse=False)
          integer_encoded = integer_encoded.reshape(len(integer_encoded), 1)
          onehot_encoder.fit(integer_encoded)

          # convert train and test output to one-hot
          train_output_int = label_encoder.transform(train_output)
          train_output = onehot_encoder.transform(train_output_int.reshape(len(train_output_int), 1))
          test_output_int = label_encoder.transform(test_output)
          test_output = onehot_encoder.transform(test_output_int.reshape(len(test_output_int), 1))

          num_classes = len(label_encoder.classes_)
          print("Number of classes: %d" % num_classes)

Number of classes: 369
```

The fit function learns which classes exist. It learns that there are 369 different class names. The tranform function turns them into integers. This is done by sorting the classes and giving each class an integer ID. integer_encoded helps to reproduce the list of classes as integer IDs. The one-hot encoder takes these integers and fits on them; this too learns how many different integers are represented. Just as LabelEncoder learned about the class names, onehot_encoder is going to learn that there are 369 different integers.

The code then moves to LabelEncoder which transforms train_output into integers. These integers are then transformed into one-hot encoding. The one-hot encoding returns a 369-dimension with the first dimension of 369 values and a vector of 369 values. All values are zeros except for a single 1. The position of this 1 depends on which class it is. test_output undergoes the same process. When the training data for input and output is ready, we proceed to build a neural network.

To do this, we are going to use `Sequential` again:

```
In [11]:  from keras.models import Sequential
          from keras.layers import Dense, Dropout, Flatten
          from keras.layers import Conv2D, MaxPooling2D
```

Sequential is a feed-forward network. Even though there are convolutions that still feed forward and are not recurrent, there are no cycles. Dense layers are used at the end of the network. We also use `Dropout` to try to prevent overfitting. When we switch from convolutions to dense layers, we need to use the `flatten` command, since convolutions are two-dimensional and dense layers are not. We also need to use `Conv2D` and `MaxPooling2D`.

The following code block is our network design:

```
In [12]:  model = Sequential()
          model.add(Conv2D(32, kernel_size=(3, 3), activation='relu',
                           input_shape=np.shape(train_input[0])))
          model.add(MaxPooling2D(pool_size=(2, 2)))
          model.add(Conv2D(32, (3, 3), activation='relu'))
          model.add(MaxPooling2D(pool_size=(2, 2)))
          model.add(Flatten())
          model.add(Dense(1024, activation='tanh'))
          model.add(Dropout(0.5))
          model.add(Dense(num_classes, activation='softmax'))

          model.compile(loss='categorical_crossentropy', optimizer='adam',
                        metrics=['accuracy'])

          print(model.summary())
```

This is modeled after MNIST design, which handles handwritten numbers. We start by making a sequential model. We need to add a convolution layer that has 32 different convolutions. The kernel size will be 3 x 3 and the activation will be ReLU. Since this is the first layer, we need to mention the input shape. If you recall, the dimensions were 30 x 30 x 3.

We use the kernel size of 3 x 3 and the stride as 1 as it is the default value. Having the stride as 1 will require padding. This is going to produce a 30 x 30 x 32 shape because there are 32 convolutions. The 30 x 30 dimensions remain constant. WE now observe that we haven't really reduced dimensions just by doing this convolution.

`MaxPooling` is used to reduce the dimensions by half. This is possible because it has a 2 x 2 pool size. We then follow with another convolution layer, which is another dimensionality reduction.

After all the convolutions have taken place, we flatten everything. This converts a two-dimensional representation into a one-dimensional representation. This is then fed into a dense layer with more than 1,000 neurons.

This dense layer will then have a `tanh` activation. This is then fed into another dense layer of neurons. This time around, there are 369 of them for the class outputs. This is the `onehot_encoding` output. We're not going to do any particular activation except for softmax. So, the original values will be rescaled to be between 0 and 1. This means that the sum of all the values across the 369 different neurons is 1.0. Softmax basically turns the output into a probability.

Proceeding to compiling `categorical _crossentropy` again helps us predict one of multiple classes. You would want to do this on the `adam` optimizer and observe it's accuracy. Here's the model's summary:

```
Layer (type)                     Output Shape              Param #
=================================================================
conv2d_1 (Conv2D)                (None, 30, 30, 32)        896

max_pooling2d_1 (MaxPooling2     (None, 15, 15, 32)        0

conv2d_2 (Conv2D)                (None, 13, 13, 32)        9248

max_pooling2d_2 (MaxPooling2     (None, 6, 6, 32)          0

flatten_1 (Flatten)              (None, 1152)              0

dense_1 (Dense)                  (None, 1024)              1180672

dropout_1 (Dropout)              (None, 1024)              0

dense_2 (Dense)                  (None, 369)               378225
=================================================================
Total params: 1,569,041
Trainable params: 1,569,041
Non-trainable params: 0
```

It is observed that the convolution layer doesn't change the dimensions, but the pooling does. It reduces it by half because of the odd dimension size, that is, 15. The next layer is at 13 output, which also gets reduced by half. The `conv2d_1 (Conv2D)` parameters are used for learning the convolutions. The `dense_1 (Dense)` parameters are used for learning the weights connected to the prior layer. In a similiar fashion, the `dense_2 (Dense)` parameters are for the weights for the prior layer. Ultimately, we have about 1.6 million parameters.

We're going to visualize the performance's accuracy and validation's accuracy with TensorBoard. We're going to save all the results into a directory called `mnist-style` because that's the style of the network we built earlier. The following is a callback:

```
In [13]:  import keras.callbacks
          tensorboard = keras.callbacks.TensorBoard(log_dir='./logs/mnist-style')
```

Keras supports callbacks of various types. The callback is used in the `fit` method, so after every epoch, it calls the callback. It passes information to the callback, such as the validation loss and the training loss. We use 10 epochs and a batch size of 32, with a 0.2, 20%, validation split.

Here's the result of the training:

```
In [14]:  model.fit(train_input, train_output,
                    batch_size=32,
                    epochs=10,
                    verbose=2,
                    validation_split=0.2,
                    callbacks=[tensorboard])

Train on 107668 samples, validate on 26918 samples
Epoch 1/10
 - 54s - loss: 1.5568 - acc: 0.6243 - val_loss: 0.9898 - val_acc: 0.7257
Epoch 2/10
 - 52s - loss: 0.9820 - acc: 0.7281 - val_loss: 0.8964 - val_acc: 0.7501
Epoch 3/10
 - 52s - loss: 0.8730 - acc: 0.7523 - val_loss: 0.8776 - val_acc: 0.7531
Epoch 4/10
 - 52s - loss: 0.8067 - acc: 0.7662 - val_loss: 0.8391 - val_acc: 0.7629
Epoch 5/10
 - 52s - loss: 0.7520 - acc: 0.7771 - val_loss: 0.8406 - val_acc: 0.7579
Epoch 6/10
 - 52s - loss: 0.7137 - acc: 0.7868 - val_loss: 0.8607 - val_acc: 0.7586
Epoch 7/10
 - 52s - loss: 0.6812 - acc: 0.7922 - val_loss: 0.8696 - val_acc: 0.7648
Epoch 8/10
 - 52s - loss: 0.6544 - acc: 0.7984 - val_loss: 0.8581 - val_acc: 0.7655
Epoch 9/10
 - 52s - loss: 0.6312 - acc: 0.8015 - val_loss: 0.8518 - val_acc: 0.7595
Epoch 10/10
 - 52s - loss: 0.6125 - acc: 0.8076 - val_loss: 0.8854 - val_acc: 0.7609
```

Now, there are a lot of choices, but ultimately we need to check them. We got about 76% validation accuracy, and when we test this out on the test set, we get the same 76% accuracy. Now, there were a lot of decisions in this design, including how many convolution layers to have and what size they should be, what kernel should be used or what size of kernel, what kind of stride, what the activation was for the convolutions, where the max pooling showed up, if it ever did, what the pooling size was, how many dense layers we have, when do they appear, what is the activation, and so on and so forth. A lot of decisions. It's quite difficult to know how to choose these different designs. These are actually called **hyperparameters**.

The weights that can be learned during the fit procedure are just called parameters, but the decisions you have to make about how to design the network and the activation functions and so forth we call hyperparameters, because they can't be learned by the network. In order to try different parameters, we can just do some loops:

```
In [17]:  # try various model configurations and parameters to find the best

          import time

          results = []
          for conv2d_count in [1, 2]:
              for dense_size in [128, 256, 512, 1024, 2048]:
                  for dropout in [0.0, 0.25, 0.50, 0.75]:
                      model = Sequential()
                      for i in range(conv2d_count):
                          if i == 0:
                              model.add(Conv2D(32, kernel_size=(3, 3), activation='relu', input_shape=np.shape(train_input[0])))
                          else:
                              model.add(Conv2D(32, kernel_size=(3, 3), activation='relu'))
                          model.add(MaxPooling2D(pool_size=(2, 2)))
                      model.add(Flatten())
                      model.add(Dense(dense_size, activation='tanh'))
                      if dropout > 0.0:
                          model.add(Dropout(dropout))
                      model.add(Dense(num_classes, activation='softmax'))

                      model.compile(loss='categorical_crossentropy', optimizer='adam', metrics=['accuracy'])

                      log_dir = './logs/conv2d_%d-dense_%d-dropout_%.2f' % (conv2d_count, dense_size, dropout)
                      tensorboard = keras.callbacks.TensorBoard(log_dir=log_dir)

                      start = time.time()
                      model.fit(train_input, train_output, batch_size=32, epochs=10,
                                verbose=0, validation_split=0.2, callbacks=[tensorboard])
                      score = model.evaluate(test_input, test_output, verbose=2)
                      end = time.time()
```

We will time how long it takes to train each of these. We will collect the results, which would be the accuracy numbers. Then, we will try a convolution 2D, which will have one or two such layers. We're going to try a dense layer with 128 neurons. We will try a dropout as `for dropout in [0.0, 0.25, 0.50, 0.7`, which will be either yes or no, and means 0-25%, 50%, 75%. So, for each of these combinations, we make a model depending on how many convolutions we're going to have, with convolution layers either one or two. We're going to add a convolution layer.

If it's the first layer, we need to put in the input shape, otherwise we'll just add the layer. Then, after adding the convolution layer, we're going to do the same with max pooling. Then, we're going to flatten and add a dense layer of whatever size that comes from `for dense_size in [128, 256, 512, 1024, 2048]: loop`. It will always be `tanh`, though.

If `Dropout` is used, we're going to add a dropout layer. Calling this dropout means, say it's 50%, that every time it goes to update the weights after each batch, there's a 50% chance for each weight that it won't be updated, but we put this between the two dense layers to kind of protect it from overfitting. The last layer will always be the number of classes because it has to be, and we'll use softmax. It gets compiled in the same way.

Set up a different log directory for TensorBoard so that we can distinguish the different configurations. Start the timer and run fit. Do the evaluation and get the score, stop the timer, and print the results. So, here it is running on all of these different configurations:

```
Conv2D count: 1, Dense size: 128, Dropout: 0.00 - Loss: 1.16, Accuracy: 0.74, Time: 419 sec
Conv2D count: 1, Dense size: 128, Dropout: 0.25 - Loss: 0.92, Accuracy: 0.76, Time: 447 sec
Conv2D count: 1, Dense size: 128, Dropout: 0.50 - Loss: 0.82, Accuracy: 0.77, Time: 452 sec
Conv2D count: 1, Dense size: 128, Dropout: 0.75 - Loss: 0.79, Accuracy: 0.77, Time: 458 sec
Conv2D count: 1, Dense size: 256, Dropout: 0.00 - Loss: 1.30, Accuracy: 0.74, Time: 430 sec
Conv2D count: 1, Dense size: 256, Dropout: 0.25 - Loss: 1.12, Accuracy: 0.76, Time: 459 sec
Conv2D count: 1, Dense size: 256, Dropout: 0.50 - Loss: 0.96, Accuracy: 0.77, Time: 461 sec
Conv2D count: 1, Dense size: 256, Dropout: 0.75 - Loss: 0.78, Accuracy: 0.78, Time: 461 sec
Conv2D count: 1, Dense size: 512, Dropout: 0.00 - Loss: 1.60, Accuracy: 0.74, Time: 440 sec
Conv2D count: 1, Dense size: 512, Dropout: 0.25 - Loss: 1.43, Accuracy: 0.75, Time: 466 sec
Conv2D count: 1, Dense size: 512, Dropout: 0.50 - Loss: 1.24, Accuracy: 0.75, Time: 471 sec
Conv2D count: 1, Dense size: 512, Dropout: 0.75 - Loss: 0.87, Accuracy: 0.77, Time: 475 sec
Conv2D count: 1, Dense size: 1024, Dropout: 0.00 - Loss: 2.13, Accuracy: 0.72, Time: 480 sec
Conv2D count: 1, Dense size: 1024, Dropout: 0.25 - Loss: 1.94, Accuracy: 0.73, Time: 517 sec
Conv2D count: 1, Dense size: 1024, Dropout: 0.50 - Loss: 1.59, Accuracy: 0.73, Time: 526 sec
Conv2D count: 1, Dense size: 1024, Dropout: 0.75 - Loss: 0.98, Accuracy: 0.76, Time: 527 sec
Conv2D count: 1, Dense size: 2048, Dropout: 0.00 - Loss: 2.00, Accuracy: 0.70, Time: 587 sec
Conv2D count: 1, Dense size: 2048, Dropout: 0.25 - Loss: 2.02, Accuracy: 0.70, Time: 629 sec
Conv2D count: 1, Dense size: 2048, Dropout: 0.50 - Loss: 1.55, Accuracy: 0.72, Time: 631 sec
Conv2D count: 1, Dense size: 2048, Dropout: 0.75 - Loss: 1.29, Accuracy: 0.73, Time: 636 sec
Conv2D count: 2, Dense size: 128, Dropout: 0.00 - Loss: 0.87, Accuracy: 0.76, Time: 531 sec
Conv2D count: 2, Dense size: 128, Dropout: 0.25 - Loss: 0.79, Accuracy: 0.77, Time: 570 sec
Conv2D count: 2, Dense size: 128, Dropout: 0.50 - Loss: 0.74, Accuracy: 0.78, Time: 568 sec
Conv2D count: 2, Dense size: 128, Dropout: 0.75 - Loss: 0.79, Accuracy: 0.77, Time: 573 sec
Conv2D count: 2, Dense size: 256, Dropout: 0.00 - Loss: 0.99, Accuracy: 0.76, Time: 550 sec
Conv2D count: 2, Dense size: 256, Dropout: 0.25 - Loss: 0.85, Accuracy: 0.77, Time: 583 sec
Conv2D count: 2, Dense size: 256, Dropout: 0.50 - Loss: 0.77, Accuracy: 0.78, Time: 579 sec
```

0.74 is the actual test set accuracy. So, you can see that there are a lot of different numbers for accuracy. They go down to low point sevens up to the high point sevens, and the time differs depending on how many parameters there are in the network. We can visualize these results because we are using the callback function.

Here's the accuracy and loss, which are from the training set:

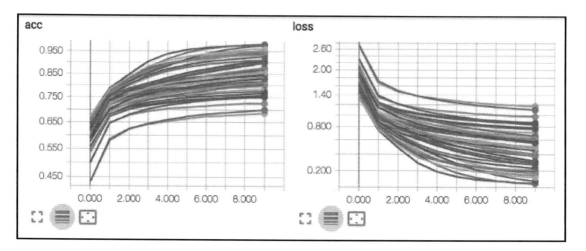

And here's the validation accuracy and validation loss:

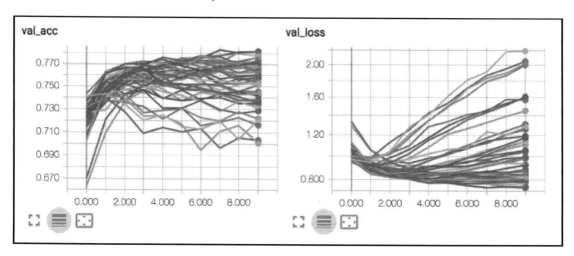

Zoom out a bit so that we can see the configurations on the side, and then we can turn them all off. Turn `mnist-style` back on. This was the first one we tried:

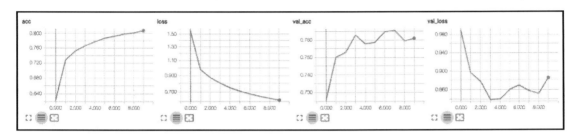

You can see that the accuracy goes up and the loss goes down. That's pretty normal. Validation accuracy goes up and loss goes down, and it mostly stays consistent. What we don't want to see is validation loss skyrocketing after a while, even though the accuracy is going way up. That's pretty much by-definition overfitting. It's learning the training examples really well, but it's getting much worse on the examples it didn't see. We really don't want that to happen. So, let's compare a few things. First, we'll compare different dropouts. Let's go to `conv2d_1-dense_128` but with different dropouts.

As far as loss goes:

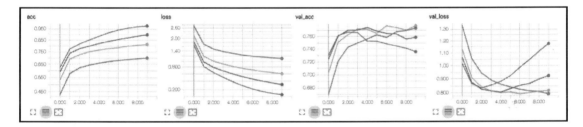

We can see that with a very low dropout, such as 0 or 0.25, the loss is minimized. That's because if you want to really learn that training set, don't refuse to update weights. Instead, update all of them all the time. With that same run, by looking at the dark blue line, we can see that it definitely overfit after just two epochs because the validation loss, the examples it did not see, started to get much worse. So, that's where the overfitting started. It's pretty clear that dropout reduces overfitting. Look at the 0.75 dropout. That's where the validation loss just got better and better, which means lower and lower.

It doesn't make it the most accurate, though, because we can see that the accuracy is not necessarily the best for our training set or the validation set:

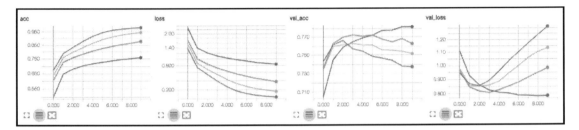

Actually, about 0.5 seems pretty good for a validation set. Now, let's just make sure it's the same for other layers. Again, with no dropouts (0.0), we get the lowest training loss but the highest validation loss. Likewise, we get a 0.75 dropout for the lowest validation loss but not necessarily the best training.

Now, let's compare how many dense layers they have. We're just going to stick with dropout 0.5, so we'll use `conv2d_1`. So, we have one convolution layer, `dense_*`, and a dropout of 0.50:

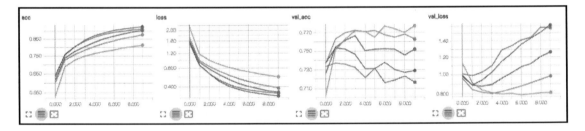

So the choice here is, does the dense layer have 128, 256, 512, 1,024, or 2,048? In the previous graph, we can see that there are some clear cases of overfitting. Pretty much anything that's not the 128 starts to suffer from overfitting. So, a dense layer of 128 is probably the best choice. Now, let's compare one convolution layer to two convolution layers:

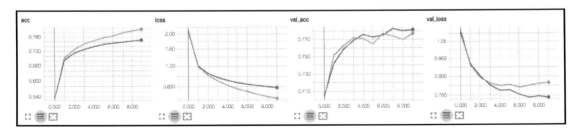

Not a big difference, actually. For validation, we get two convolution layers and receive the lowest loss, which is usually the same as the highest accuracy. This means that we've narrowed down. This is called model selection, which is all about figuring out what the best model is, as well as the best hyperparameters. We've narrowed this down to the two-dimensional convolution, two layers of that, 128 dense in the first dense layer, and 50% dropout. Given that, let's retrain on all the data so that we have the best trained model we could possibly have:

```
In [22]:   # rebuild/retrain a model with the best parameters (from the search) and use all data
           model = Sequential()
           model.add(Conv2D(32, kernel_size=(3, 3), activation='relu', input_shape=np.shape(train_input[0])))
           model.add(MaxPooling2D(pool_size=(2, 2)))
           model.add(Conv2D(32, (3, 3), activation='relu'))
           model.add(MaxPooling2D(pool_size=(2, 2)))
           model.add(Flatten())
           model.add(Dense(128, activation='tanh'))
           model.add(Dropout(0.5))
           model.add(Dense(num_classes, activation='softmax'))
           model.compile(loss='categorical_crossentropy', optimizer='adam', metrics=['accuracy'])
           print(model.summary())
           # join train and test data so we train the network on all data we have available to us
           model.fit(np.concatenate((train_input, test_input)),
                     np.concatenate((train_output, test_output)),
                     batch_size=32, epochs=10, verbose=2)

           # save the trained model
           model.save("mathsymbols.model")

           # save label encoder (to reverse one-hot encoding)
           np.save('classes.npy', label_encoder.classes_)
```

We get our two convolution layers, we do our dense 128 dropout 0.5, and in this case we take all the data we have, the entire dataset trained and tested, and stick it all together. Now, we can't really evaluate this model because we just lost our testing set, so what we're going to do instead is use this model to predict other images. Actually, we're going to save the model after it's fit and we're going to show how to load in a minute. If you're going to load this in another file, you're also going to want to know what those labels were called because all we know is the one-hot encoding. From the one-hot encoding, we can get back the integer number, but still that's not the same as the actual name of the symbol. So, we have to save the classes from `LabelEncoder` and we're just going to use a `numpy` file to save that.

Let's train the model:

Layer (type)	Output Shape	Param #
conv2d_68 (Conv2D)	(None, 30, 30, 32)	896

This could actually be all in a separate file. You can load everything again:

```
In [32]: # load the pre-trained model and predict the math symbol for an arbitrary image;
         # the code below could be placed in a separate file

         import keras.models
         model2 = keras.models.load_model("mathsymbols.model")
         print(model2.summary())

         # restore the class name to integer encoder
         label_encoder2 = LabelEncoder()
         label_encoder2.classes_ = np.load('classes.npy')

         def predict(img_path):
             newimg = keras.preprocessing.image.img_to_array(pil_image.open(img_path))
             newimg /= 255.0

             # do the prediction
             prediction = model2.predict(newimg.reshape(1, 32, 32, 3))

             # figure out which output neuron had the highest score, and reverse the one-hot encoding
             inverted = label_encoder2.inverse_transform([np.argmax(prediction)]) # argmax finds highest-scoring output
             print("Prediction: %s, confidence: %.2f" % (inverted[0], np.max(prediction)))
```

Import `keras.models` and you can use the `load _model` feature. The model file there actually saves the structure as well as the weights. That's all you need to do to recover the network. You can print the summary again. For `LabelEncoder`, we need to call the constructor again and give it the classes that we saved ahead of time.

Now, we can make a function called predict takes an image. We do a little bit of preprocessing to turn the image into an array, we divide it by 255, and we predict. If you have a whole set of images, you won't need to do this reshape, but since we just have one, we can put it in an array that has a single row. We will get the prediction out of this, and using `LabelEncoder`, we can reverse the prediction to the actual name of the class, the name of the symbol, and which prediction? Well, it's one-hot encoding, so you can figure out the position of the highest number. This takes all the neuron outputs, the 369, figures out what the largest confidence number is, and says that's the one that was predicted. Therefore, one-hot encoding would tell you this particular symbol, and then we can print it:

```
Layer (type)                  Output Shape            Param #
=================================================================
conv2d_68 (Conv2D)            (None, 30, 30, 32)      896

max_pooling2d_68 (MaxPooling  (None, 15, 15, 32)      0

conv2d_69 (Conv2D)            (None, 13, 13, 32)      9248

max_pooling2d_69 (MaxPooling  (None, 6, 6, 32)        0

flatten_45 (Flatten)          (None, 1152)            0

dense_89 (Dense)              (None, 128)             147584

dropout_34 (Dropout)          (None, 128)             0

dense_90 (Dense)              (None, 369)             47601
=================================================================
Total params: 205,329
```

Here's how we can use that function:

```
In [33]:   # grab an image (we'll just use a random training image for demonstration purposes)
           predict("HASYv2/hasy-data/v2-00010.png")

           Prediction: A, confidence: 0.87

In [34]:   predict("HASYv2/hasy-data/v2-00500.png")

           Prediction: \pi, confidence: 0.58

In [35]:   predict("HASYv2/hasy-data/v2-00700.png")

           Prediction: \alpha, confidence: 0.88
```

We're actually using the training images for this purpose instead of making new ones, but you get the idea. You take an image that says that's an A, and I'm 87% confident about it. For pi prediction, we're 58% confident and for alpha prediction, we're 88% confident. Next, we'll look at the bird species example we used previously, and instead of using all of the attributes that humans created, we're going to use the images themselves.

Revisiting the bird species identifier to use images

In this section, we're going to revisit the bird species identifier from before. This time, we're going to update it to use neural networks and deep learning. Can you recall the birds dataset? It has 200 different species of birds across 12,000 images. Unlike last time, we won't be using the human-labeled attributes, and instead we'll use the actual images without any pre-processing. In our first attempt, we're going to build a custom convolutional neural network, just like we did for the mathematical symbols classifier.

Let's go to the code. We will start with the typical imports:

```
In [1]:  import numpy as np
         from keras.models import Sequential, load_model
         from keras.layers import Dropout, Flatten, Conv2D, MaxPooling2D, Dense, Activation
         from keras.utils import np_utils
         from keras.preprocessing.image import ImageDataGenerator
         from keras.callbacks import TensorBoard
         import itertools

         Using TensorFlow backend.
```

We'll make some convenience variables, the rows and columns of the image, the width and height, and the number of channels, RGB, though every bird image will be equal. Even though they're not all necessarily the same size, we're going to resize them to this size so that they're all consistent:

```
In [2]:  # all images will be converted to this size
         ROWS = 256
         COLS = 256
         CHANNELS = 3
```

Now, this project introduces an interesting feature on Keras called an **image data generator**:

```
In [3]: train_image_generator = ImageDataGenerator(horizontal_flip=True, rescale=1./255, rotation_range=45)
        test_image_generator = ImageDataGenerator(horizontal_flip=False, rescale=1./255, rotation_range=0)

        train_generator = train_image_generator.flow_from_directory('train', target_size=(ROWS, COLS), class_mode='categorical')
        test_generator = test_image_generator.flow_from_directory('test', target_size=(ROWS, COLS), class_mode='categorical')

        Found 5994 images belonging to 200 classes.
        Found 5794 images belonging to 200 classes.
```

The data generator can produce new images from the existing training set and these new images can have various differences; for example, they can be rotated, they can be flipped horizontally or vertically, and so forth. Then, we can generate more examples than we actually started with. This is a great thing to do when you have a small number of training examples. We have, in our case, about 6,000 training sets. That's relatively small in deep learning, so we want to be able to generate more; the data generator will just keep generating them as long as we keep asking for them. For the training images, we want to also generate versions with the horizontal flip. We don't want to do a vertical flip because I don't expect any bird images to be upside down. We also want to support rotations of up to 45 degrees, and we want to rescale all the pixel values to divide by 255. Actually, ImageDataGenerator just calls the constructor, so nothing's actually happened yet. What you want to do next is use flow_from_directory, so that your images can be organized into directories or subdirectories.

We have a train directory, and inside that there's going to be a folder for each bird class. So, there's 200 different folders inside train and inside those folders are the images for that particular bird. We want all the images to be resized to 256 x 256 and we can indicate that instead of using binary, we want to use categorical classes, meaning that we will have lots of different classes (200, in this case). We're going to use the data generator for the test set too, just because flow_from_directory is a convenient function. We don't want to do any flips, though, or rotations. We just want to use the testing set as is so we can compare it with other people. The other really convenient thing about flow_from _directory is that it's automatically going to produce a numpy matrix with the image data, and it's also going to give the class values in one-hot encoding.

So, what was several steps before is now being done all at once.

Now, I don't really need to do a reset, but since these are technically iterators, if you're constantly fixing the model and trying to retrain, then you might want to do a reset so that you get all the same images in the same order. In any event, it's an iterator, so you can call next, reset, and so forth:

```
In [12]:  train_generator.reset()
          test_generator.reset()

          model = Sequential()
          model.add(Conv2D(64, (3,3), input_shape=(ROWS, COLS, CHANNELS)))
          model.add(Activation('relu'))
          model.add(Conv2D(64, (3,3)))
          model.add(Activation('relu'))
          model.add(MaxPooling2D(pool_size=(4,4)))
          model.add(Conv2D(64, (3,3)))
          model.add(Activation('relu'))
          model.add(Conv2D(64, (3,3)))
          model.add(Activation('relu'))
          model.add(MaxPooling2D(pool_size=(4,4)))
          model.add(Flatten())
          model.add(Dropout(0.5))
          model.add(Dense(400))
          model.add(Activation('relu'))
          model.add(Dropout(0.5))
          model.add(Dense(200))
          model.add(Activation('softmax'))

          model.compile(loss='categorical_crossentropy', optimizer='adamax', metrics=['accuracy'])

          model.summary()
```

Now, we will build a sequential model, which is going to be a convolutional model. We have a convolution kernel of 3 x 3, 64 of this. We also have a `relu` and another convolution built by `relu`, which we can do a max pooling with, and just from experimentation, I discovered that this works relatively well: 3 x 3 followed by 3 x 3, each 64. By having a pretty dramatic max point of 4 x 4, so we repeat this process and then we flatten. We have a dropout of 50% just to reduce overfitting, a dense of 400 neurons, another dropout, and then 200 for the output because there are 200 different classes, and because it's categorical one-hot encoding, we want to use softmax so that only one of those 200 has the highest value. We also want to ensure that they all add up to 1.0.

Here's the summary of the model. Ultimately, we have about 5 million parameters:

```
Layer (type)                     Output Shape           Param #
=================================================================
conv2d_19 (Conv2D)               (None, 254, 254, 64)    1792

activation_28 (Activation)       (None, 254, 254, 64)    0

conv2d_20 (Conv2D)               (None, 252, 252, 64)    36928

activation_29 (Activation)       (None, 252, 252, 64)    0

max_pooling2d_10 (MaxPooling     (None, 63, 63, 64)      0

conv2d_21 (Conv2D)               (None, 61, 61, 64)      36928

activation_30 (Activation)       (None, 61, 61, 64)      0

conv2d_22 (Conv2D)               (None, 59, 59, 64)      36928

activation_31 (Activation)       (None, 59, 59, 64)      0

max_pooling2d_11 (MaxPooling     (None, 14, 14, 64)      0

flatten_5 (Flatten)              (None, 12544)           0

dropout_8 (Dropout)              (None, 12544)           0

dense_9 (Dense)                  (None, 400)             5018000
```

```
activation_32 (Activation)       (None, 400)             0

dropout_9 (Dropout)              (None, 400)             0

dense_10 (Dense)                 (None, 200)             80200

activation_33 (Activation)       (None, 200)             0
=================================================================
Total params: 5,210,776
Trainable params: 5,210,776
Non-trainable params: 0
```

The different variations I did that had far more parameters, such as, say, 100 million performed worse because there were just too many parameters. There's either too many parameters, meaning it's really hard to train it to learn anything because obviously all the parameters start random, so it's really hard to make those parameters trend toward the right values, or there are so few that it's not going to learn anything either. There's kind of a balance that you have to find, and 5 million, I think, is somewhere near that balance.

Now, if you use a generator, you don't have all the data for the training prepared ahead of time; it's going to produce those images as it goes:

```
In [15]:  tensorboard = TensorBoard(log_dir='./logs/custom')

          model.fit_generator(train_generator, steps_per_epoch=512, epochs=10, callbacks=[tensorboard], verbose=2)
```

That makes it actually quite memory-efficient. You don't have to load the whole dataset ahead of time. It'll just make it as needed, but you have to call `fit _generator` instead of just using fit. What you give instead of the train input and train output is the generator. The generator knows how to produce the image matrices and it knows how to produce one-hot encoding. So, again, that's extremely convenient when you have images. There's other kinds of generators, too. Look at the Keras documentation for these.
`steps_per_epoch` shows how many images to produce per epoch, or how many batches to produce. The generator, by default, produces batches of 32 images. Regarding the number of epochs, and if you want to do some statistics on TensorBoard, you can set up a callback and verbose 2 so that we can see some output here.

There are 10 epochs:

```
         Epoch 1/10
          - 434s - loss: 4.4682 - acc: 0.0687
         Epoch 2/10
          - 440s - loss: 4.1851 - acc: 0.0919
         Epoch 3/10
          - 443s - loss: 3.9278 - acc: 0.1270
         Epoch 4/10
          - 428s - loss: 3.6948 - acc: 0.1615
         Epoch 5/10
          - 437s - loss: 3.4944 - acc: 0.1935
         Epoch 6/10
          - 439s - loss: 3.3103 - acc: 0.2196
         Epoch 7/10
          - 438s - loss: 3.1253 - acc: 0.2492
         Epoch 8/10
          - 443s - loss: 2.9927 - acc: 0.2757
         Epoch 9/10
          - 431s - loss: 2.8474 - acc: 0.2998
         Epoch 10/10
          - 430s - loss: 2.7354 - acc: 0.3271
Out[15]:  <keras.callbacks.History at 0x7fe46c531be0>
```

We can see that the training accuracy is on the images that is training on. It's not very accurate for what the accuracy is going to be on the test set, so we do this separately. The test images are also in a generator. You don't just evaluate—you use `evaluate_generator` and you say, *how many images do you want to evaluate?* We'll just do 1,000, and we'll get 22% accuracy.

That's not so bad. Random guessing would yield 0.5%, so 22% is pretty good, and that's just from a handcrafted model starting from scratch that had to learn everything from those bird images. The reason I'm saying things like this is because the next thing we're going to do is extend a pre-trained model to get a good boost in accuracy.

This model was built by hand, but it would be even better to extend something such as `Inceptionv3`, which is shown here:

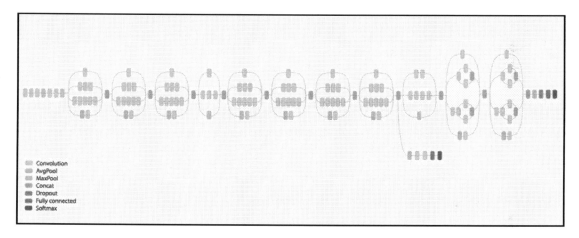

It's quite deep; it has a lot of convolutional layers and, like most CNNs, it ends with a fully-connected layer or perhaps multiple fully connected layers. The `Inceptionv3` model was designed for ImageNet. Well, it's the dataset, and there's competitions associated with it where there are millions of images and 1,000 different classes, such as insects, houses, cars, and so on. The `Inceptionv3` model is state-of-the-art, or it was at one point. It was ImageNet's competition to combat other databases. We're going to use most of this network all the way up until the fully-connected layers. We don't want the final fully-connected or dense layers because those are designed for ImageNet. Specifically, there are 1,000 outputs and that's not good for us. We don't need to recognize the ImageNet images. We do need to recognize our bird images however, and there's only 200 different classes.

So, we just chop off the front of that and replace it with our own fully-connected layer, or multiple layers. We're going to use all the convolutions that it learned, and all of the kernels that it learned based on those ImageNet images. Let's go to the code. To do this, import `Inceptionv3` from Keras's applications. There's other models that you can choose from that Keras has available as well:

```
In [1]: import numpy as np
        from keras.applications.inception_v3 import InceptionV3
        from keras.models import Sequential, load_model, Model
        from keras.layers import Input, Dropout, Flatten, Conv2D, MaxPooling2D, Dense, Activation, GlobalAveragePooling2D
        from keras.optimizers import SGD
        from keras.utils import np_utils
        from keras.preprocessing.image import ImageDataGenerator
        from keras.callbacks import TensorBoard
        import itertools

        Using TensorFlow backend.
```

We're going to use the data generator just like we did previously.

This is where it starts to become different:

```
In [4]: # create the base pre-trained model
        base_model = InceptionV3(weights='imagenet', include_top=False)

        # add a global spatial average pooling layer
        x = base_model.output
        x = GlobalAveragePooling2D()(x)
        # add a fully-connected layer
        x = Dense(1024, activation='relu')(x)
        out_layer = Dense(200, activation='softmax')(x)

        # this is the model we will train
        model = Model(inputs=base_model.input, outputs=out_layer)
```

First, load the `InceptionV3` model using the ImageNet weights. `include_top =False` means to drop off the dense fully connected layers at the top. That's what they call the top. That's where it finally produces 1,000 different outputs. We don't want that. We want just the convolutions. This would be called the `base_model`. Call x, which is the output of the base model, add a `GlobalAveragePooling`, which means that it's computing the average across the whole convolution, and then put in some dense layers, with 1,024 dense neurons and another layer of 200. Of course, the 200 is because we have 200 different bird species, and the 1,024 is just to learn how the convolutions can match the bird species and then produce a model with those layers. The input of the model is the input of `Inceptionv3` and the output is `out_layer = Dense(200, activation='softmax')(x)`.

At this point, you can call regular model functions such as compile, but before we compile, we want to mark all of the base model layers and all of the convolutions as not trainable.

We're going to perform two steps here. When we attached our new two dense layers, the 1,024 dense and the 200 dense, those have random weights, so they're pretty much useless so far. The convolutions have been learned on ImageNet, so they're good. We don't want to change the convolutions below all those kernels by training on our bird images until we get that new pair of dense layers in the right order. So, we're first going to mark those layers from the inception model as not trainable; just keep those numbers as they are—we're only going to train our two new layers:

```
In [5]:  # first: train only the top layers (which were randomly initialized)
         # i.e. freeze all convolutional InceptionV3 layers
         for layer in base_model.layers:
             layer.trainable = False

         model.compile(loss='categorical_crossentropy', optimizer='rmsprop', metrics=['accuracy'])

         model.summary()
```

Layer (type)	Output Shape	Param #	Connected to
input_1 (InputLayer)	(None, None, None, 3	0	
conv2d_1 (Conv2D)	(None, None, None, 3	864	input_1[0][0]
batch_normalization_1 (BatchNor	(None, None, None, 3	96	conv2d_1[0][0]
activation_1 (Activation)	(None, None, None, 3	0	batch_normalization_1[0][0]

That happens next on the fit generator, just like before.

We will do 100 epochs to start off:

```
In [6]:  tensorboard = TensorBoard(log_dir='./logs')

         model.fit_generator(train_generator, steps_per_epoch=32, epochs=100, callbacks=[tensorboard], verbose=2)
         Epoch 90/100
          - 26s - loss: 1.5382 - acc: 0.5576
         Epoch 91/100
          - 26s - loss: 1.3803 - acc: 0.6133
         Epoch 92/100
          - 25s - loss: 1.5539 - acc: 0.5556
         Epoch 93/100
          - 26s - loss: 1.5569 - acc: 0.5703
         Epoch 94/100
          - 25s - loss: 1.4826 - acc: 0.5791
         Epoch 95/100
          - 26s - loss: 1.5378 - acc: 0.5586
         Epoch 96/100
          - 26s - loss: 1.5142 - acc: 0.5947
         Epoch 97/100
          - 26s - loss: 1.4756 - acc: 0.5762
         Epoch 98/100
          - 26s - loss: 1.4465 - acc: 0.6025
         Epoch 99/100
          - 26s - loss: 1.5138 - acc: 0.5820
```

And we'll do an evaluation:

```
In [7]:  print(model.evaluate_generator(test_generator, steps=5000))
         [2.3260338047121207, 0.44336327658772534]
```

So, now, we're up to 44% accuracy. So just by using the inception v3 weights and structure or ImageNet but replacing the top two layers with our own fully-connected network, we get a 20% boost from what we had with our own custom convolutional neural network. But we can do even better.

We can use what we just got so that the model has now trained the top two layers and marked everything as trainable:

```
In [8]:  # unfreeze all layers for more training
         for layer in model.layers:
             layer.trainable = True

         # we need to recompile the model for these modifications to take effect
         # we use SGD with a low learning rate
         model.compile(optimizer=SGD(lr=0.0001, momentum=0.9), loss='categorical_crossentropy', metrics=['accuracy'])

         model.fit_generator(train_generator, steps_per_epoch=32, epochs=100)
Epoch 90/100
32/32 [==============================] - 27s 859ms/step - loss: 0.3098 - acc: 0.9180
Epoch 91/100
32/32 [==============================] - 27s 846ms/step - loss: 0.2865 - acc: 0.9268
Epoch 92/100
32/32 [==============================] - 27s 852ms/step - loss: 0.2902 - acc: 0.9141
Epoch 93/100
32/32 [==============================] - 27s 832ms/step - loss: 0.2934 - acc: 0.9227
Epoch 94/100
32/32 [==============================] - 28s 860ms/step - loss: 0.2731 - acc: 0.9307
Epoch 95/100
32/32 [==============================] - 27s 845ms/step - loss: 0.2777 - acc: 0.9195
```

So, now that the top two layers are kind of massaged into a form that is reasonable, with 44% accuracy, we're going to let the entire network update all of our bird images. We're going to do it very slowly using stochastic gradient descent with a very slow learning rate and a high momentum. Going through 100 epochs, we now have 64%:

```
In [9]:  test_generator.reset()
         print(model.evaluate_generator(test_generator, steps=5000))
         [1.4155961280392264, 0.63971983164771662]
```

So, we basically did a 20% boost each time. With the custom CNN, we got 22% accuracy just by starting from scratch. Now, of course, this is not as big of a network as the inception model, but it kind of shows what happens if you just start from scratch. Then, we started with inception, all the kernels, but then added our own random 2 layers on top, with random weights, trained those weights but did not change the kernels, and we got 44% accuracy. Finally, we went through and updated all the weights, kernels, and the top layer, and we got 64% accuracy.

So, this is far far better than what random guessing would be, which is 0.5%, and it's been an increasing gain in accuracy each time we've improved the model. You can save the result and then you can load it into a separate file, perhaps by loading the model:

```
In [10]:  model.save("birds-inceptionv3.model")
```

You also want to know what the class names are if you want to print the name of the bird to the user:

```
In [1]:  from keras.models import load_model
         from keras.preprocessing import image
         from os import listdir
         import numpy as np

         Using TensorFlow backend.

In [2]:  ROWS = 256
         COLS = 256

In [3]:  CLASS_NAMES = sorted(listdir('images'))    I

         model = load_model('birds-inceptionv3.model')
```

In this case, we can just list the subdirectories in a sorted form because that's going to match the one -hot encoding, and we can define a function called `predict` where you give it a filename with an image in it and it loads that image. Make sure it resizes it and converts it into an array, divides it by 255, and then runs the predictor. All this was done for us before with the image generator:

```
In [4]:  def predict(fname):
             img = image.load_img(fname, target_size=(ROWS, COLS))
             img_tensor = image.img_to_array(img) # (height, width, channels)
             # (1, height, width, channels), add a dimension because the model expects this shape:
             # (batch_size, height, width, channels)
             img_tensor = np.expand_dims(img_tensor, axis=0)
             img_tensor /= 255. # model expects values in the range [0, 1]
             prediction = model.predict(img_tensor)[0]
             best_score_index = np.argmax(prediction)
             bird = CLASS_NAMES[best_score_index] # retrieve original class name
             print("Prediction: %s (%.2f%%)" % (bird, 100*prediction[best_score_index]))
```

But now, because we're doing this one at a time, we're just going to do it by hand instead. Run the prediction, find out what the best score was, the position, and retrieve the class name and then print it, plus the confidence. There's a couple of examples of just birds that I found on the internet:

```
In [5]:  predict('test-birds/annas_hummingbird_sim_1.jpg')
         predict('test-birds/house_wren.jpg')
         predict('test-birds/canada_goose_1.jpg')

         Prediction: 067.Anna_Hummingbird (98.76%)
         Prediction: 196.House_Wren (47.01%)
         Prediction: 071.Long_tailed_Jaeger (37.12%)
```

I can't guarantee that these were not part of the training set, but who knows. In the case of the hummingbird, they got it right. The house wren was also predicted correctly. However, the goose was not predicted correctly. This is an example of letting the user type in filenames. So if you have your own images that are relatively close to photography type images, you should consider using a pre-trained model like `InceptionV3` to get a major gain in accuracy.

Summary

In this chapter, we discussed deep learning and CNNs. We practiced with convolutional neural networks and deep learning with two projects. First, we built a system that can read handwritten mathematical symbols and then revisited the bird species identifier form and changed the implementation to use a deep convolutional neural network that is significantly more accurate. This concludes the Python AI projects for beginners.

Other Books You May Enjoy

If you enjoyed this book, you may be interested in these other books by Packt:

Artificial Intelligence By Example
Denis Rothman

ISBN: 9781788990547

- Use adaptive thinking to solve real-life AI case studies
- Rise beyond being a modern-day factory code worker
- Acquire advanced AI, machine learning, and deep learning designing skills
- Learn about cognitive NLP chatbots, quantum computing, and IoT and blockchain technology
- Understand future AI solutions and adapt quickly to them
- Develop out-of-the-box thinking to face any challenge the market presents

Artificial Intelligence with Python
Prateek Joshi

ISBN: 9781786464392

- Realize different classification and regression techniques
- Understand the concept of clustering and how to use it to automatically segment data
- See how to build an intelligent recommender system
- Understand logic programming and how to use it
- Build automatic speech recognition systems
- Understand the basics of heuristic search and genetic programming
- Develop games using Artificial Intelligence
- Learn how reinforcement learning works
- Discover how to build intelligent applications centered on images, text, and time series data
- See how to use deep learning algorithms and build applications based on it

Leave a review - let other readers know what you think

Please share your thoughts on this book with others by leaving a review on the site that you bought it from. If you purchased the book from Amazon, please leave us an honest review on this book's Amazon page. This is vital so that other potential readers can see and use your unbiased opinion to make purchasing decisions, we can understand what our customers think about our products, and our authors can see your feedback on the title that they have worked with Packt to create. It will only take a few minutes of your time, but is valuable to other potential customers, our authors, and Packt. Thank you!

Index